'Swans and cygnets'.   *Reproduced by courtesy of W.R. Royle Ltd.*

VERNON WARD
Child of the Edwardian Era

Josephine Walpole

Antique Collectors' Club

ISBN 1 85149 077 9

Published for the Antique Collectors' Club
by the Antique Collectors' Club Ltd.

British Library CIP Data
Walpole, Josephine
  Vernon Ward
  1. English graphic arts. Ward, Vernon
  I. Title   II. Antique Collectors' Club
760′ 092′4

Printed in England by the Antique Collectors' Club Ltd.
5 Church Street, Woodbridge, Suffolk

Acknowledgements

The Editor would like to thank all those who have contributed to this book and
those who have kindly helped with illustrations. Special thanks are due to 'Becky'
Groombridge at whose instigation it all came about, and Julian Royle who has
been a constant help and support; thanks also to John Ward, R.A., Noël Napier-
Ford, Noël Syers, Laura Dance, Colonel and Mrs Ferguson, Kay and Hugh
Jones, Jacqueline Meyer, Royle Publications, The Medici Society, Messrs.
Solomon and Whitehead, W.N. Sharpe Limited, the Fine Art Trade Guild and,
not least, the Antique Collectors' Club for their time, care and patience.

Contents

FOREWORD
by John Ward, R.A.

This century will ever be remembered for the mountains of art schools which produced the smallest of mice. True there will be mountains of leathery pictures of Cézanne apples, mountains of sad portrayals of tired, ancient models with their dismal forms tediously and clumsily copied (since skill was not an 'in' thing), and heaps of dull 'Men at Work' or 'The Backyard' at its most significant dismalness. This is what has been respectable from early this century and it still lingers on. Abstraction has made the little skill required for these poor products unnecessary and size knows no bounds now for acres of scrawls clutter the art schools.

This situation came about because it was thought to be more respectable for painters to live by teaching rather than by painting and selling their work. By teaching, the horrid fact of having to produce work that was wanted was avoided. Vernon Ward was an original, a nonconformer, and he flew in the face of these respectabilities. He had grown up in the shadow of a father who earned his living by selling pictures, a precarious business; his student days ended with the great depression and desperation drove him to seek where his considerable gifts and skills could be best employed to keep body and soul together. His absolute honesty compelled him to declare in paint the things he loved and the places which gave comfort and joy in those dark, hard days.

First sunshine, that unreliable commodity in England: he discovered he could clear the sky of clouds and strike the exact tones which sunlight brings to buildings, trees and flowers. The sadness of towns made people yearn for the seaside villages, cottages, gardens and ships — escapism, of course — but many good artists have flourished beneath this umbrella and is it any more escapism than the academic sterility of the Cézanne still life or the sad life room?

Vernon Ward had a talent and a touch for what was most popular. This, it is sometimes thought, can be easily analysed and easily reproduced but strangely it is not so. The ingredients can be assembled and mixed but a spark is still needed, an outrageous skill and fire, which is most rare. Vernon Ward should have spawned hundreds of imitators but he did not since his skill and ingenuity were exceptional, and no cynicism drew him to his subject matter; he revelled in the prettiness of flowers, relishing the fact that prettiness was not the 'thing' — it outraged the dour, the dull, the respectable painters. He found grounds for his skill amongst the places and objects that gave people pleasure and people responded and bought. His pictures were reproduced worldwide and his name became a household word.

These were his rewards, for honours had he none; he was 'beyond the pale' and this suited his highly individualist nature. His keen intelligence told him of the foolishness of the art world which dishes out the honours, of the higher and higher stockades which critics seek to place round contemporary painting wherein they may be forever in command and forever seeking fresh idiocies to make this community safe from common understanding.

Yet he is safe. Anyone who writes about life between 1930 and 1980, of what people lived with and what gave pleasure, cannot deny him his due as the great popular painter of his time. The escapism that people find in flowers and sunshine is fundamental as is the admiration of the skill to dash at these subjects. Popular sense has a way of dishing the specialist and perceiving the character who turned his back on what is the 'done' thing — it has a healthy respect for what is thought vulgar and yet has achieved that extremely rare thing — universal popularity.

Vernon Ward was my cousin and it gives me great pleasure to write this introduction to a book which sets out to record his life and work.

Editor's note: John Ward is recognized as being one of the most brilliantly skilful of contemporary painters, a real master of his craft. He has been painting for the Royal Family since 1962 and is a favourite painter, and mentor, of Prince Charles; the two have painted together on many occasions including time spent working with watercolours aboard 'Britannia'. During the Royal Wedding, John Ward was sketching away, unobtrusively, from the choir stalls, later producing a painting which, like his portrait of the Princess of Wales, hangs in the couple's private collection.

John Ward's Exhibition at the Maas Gallery in December 1985 was an unforgettable experience — the very best of British painting in its truest sense.

Introduction

Not so many years ago it was fashionable rather to despise the Vernon Wards of this world. Many talented artists, while simply earning a living until a certain reputation was established, were known largely through the medium of cheap inferior reproductions adorning trays, wastepaper baskets, chocolate boxes and the like, and were belittled by those who fell for the gimmicks of the pseudo avant-garde who dubbed any form of meaningless abstraction 'the artist's self-expression'. Unfairly the works of the conventional painter who was unable and unwilling to jump on this unrealistic bandwagon, were consigned to the suburban semi, cheap prints in cheap white frames alongside the flying china ducks and barbola decorated mirrors, and identified with the people who lived there.

Vernon Beauvoir Ward was born to be a painter; there were no problems with dissenting parents, on the contrary his father had prayed for a son who would be interested in the arts. The two older boys detested all things artistic but Vernon took naturally to drawing and painting and from the time he could read, he read everything he could lay his hands on about art and artists.

His father, Albert Ward, was an antiquarian dealer, picture restorer and framer. Although he specialised in 17th century Dutch painting, in his shop Vernon learned to copy all schools of painting; he mixed with many and diverse artists, avidly drinking in all that they could teach him, and in this he received every possible help and encouragement from his father. The latter employed the artist, George Fox, a former R.A. student who shared his love of art and Charles Dickens, and combined the two by illustrating many Dickensian subjects for him. He taught the young Vernon a very great deal, becoming an important part of the artistic environment in which he lived and which had such a profound influence on his future.

At the tender age of fourteen and a half, the great Professor Tonks was so impressed by the precocious talent of the young Vernon that he persuaded his father to enter him as a Slade student. Tonks always maintained that a real artist could not start early enough and as for education — ''an artist educates himself''. At the Slade, as in his father's business, Vernon was given every possible encouragement, working under a number of eminent teacher-painters and, during his three years there, receiving a thorough training. It was the death of his father (of tuberculosis) when he was only twenty-one that necessitated his earning a living for himself and his mother in a rather more immediate way than building up a reputation as an artist in the purest sense.

To me and no doubt to many others who can recognise a painter for what he really is and not for what the ravages of commercialism make of him, this was the tragedy of Vernon Ward's life even to the extent, years later, of precluding him from exhibiting in certain galleries who refused to display the work of such a 'commercial' artist, however good it was. Vernon himself wrote of ''grubbing

about for any sort of commercial work — designing ladies' scarves, music covers, hotel brochures, gaslight and coke company advertising — I have made it my trade''. Later in life as he became yet more cynical he wrote of himself as ''an innocent dupe, ruthlessly exploited by the Fine Art publishing trade''. His mother was known to have burst into tears on learning that in spite of his outstanding natural talent and superb art training, he had become 'a chocolate box artist', a term applied to the lowest form of artistic life.

Thankfully, the quality of fine art reproduction has improved so dramatically in recent years that published prints and greeting cards of Vernon's work do give a much better impression of its quality while memories of the earlier 'hack' work are eventually fading away. Since his death his original work has been more fully appreciated and the time is coming when the name of Vernon Ward will be that of a very professional, traditional painter, far, far away from the 'chocolate box' image. Added to this, the mad period is nearly over. The public have seen through the gimmicks and, as always, quality raises its head again at the end of the periodic phases of insanity known temporarily as art.

That Vernon himself was fully aware of this before he died is confirmed in a letter to Julian Royle dated August 1978 and from which (with permission) I quote: ''...now when the silly 'experimentation' has died its inevitable mouldering death. 'Bricks' at the Tate — price £400 plus INSTRUCTIONS on HOW to put them on the Gallery floor! Filth exhibited in the Pall Mall Gallery; taxpayers' money used to promote the decadence of a 'caring' society.

''The mindless verbiage spewed out by the real artists (i.e. the critics) is faltering to a timid halt as staggering prices received in and at the pearly gates of artistic nirvana, namely Sotheby's and Christie's — I am amused at the 'appreciation' albeit grudgingly as it does involve a bit of face saving — of Millais, Landseer, etc. etc. etc. Cherry Ripe is ripe indeed and Munnings can rest in his grave. Millais' tears (of frustration) can now evaporate as Bubbles charmingly depicts a boyhood free of the stigma of his innocent delight in blowing bubbles instead of wrecking telephone boxes or bashing old age pensioners, a favourite pastime in between football sessions!

''If the sentiments of the old time painters sound mawkish in the ears of a violence hardened, disillusioned, apathetic, Godless society it is the explainers and the 'carers' — sociologists, pyschiatrists, weak magistrates, compassionate Judges, who have to bear some responsibility for the chaos we see everywhere — in the media and its monument, the ghastly high rise concrete blocks. The 'designers' should be compelled to try and exist in them for at least three years.''

. . . .

Vernon Ward was a prolific writer as well as artist and like many other artists had the ability to paint in words as well as pigments. His letters were a joy — never would he have subscribed to the notion that letter writing is a dying art. Sadly it was late in his life when I received my first letter from him — totally unexpectedly he wrote of his pleasure in my biography of Anna Zinkeisen. Now, equally unexpectedly, I have been asked to prepare a similar tribute to Vernon.

Like so many others he had completely fallen under Anna's spell — to him with her "sweet womanly presence" she conjured up visions of "warm June nights, moonlight and roses", the personification of all that was feminine and beautiful. With the warm generosity of one true artist towards another, he thanked me for perpetuating her memory and told me how her work had always been an inspiration to him. Many years ago, Anna sponsored Vernon in his application for election to the R.O.I., which, unfortunately and perhaps unfairly, was turned down. Even after all those years, Vernon told me bitterly, "The usual result — anybody but not Vernon Ward!"

Sifting through Vernon's papers I discovered that he started his own autobiography at least half a dozen times, each time writing in great detail of his Edwardian childhood, adding something or taking something away. The Edwardian era always had a nostalgic fascination for him — he hated so much of life in the nineteen seventies but his vivid memories of every detail of his early life indicate the extent to which, particularly as he grew older, he lived in a rose coloured past.

It was difficult to decide how best to present these autobiographical writings. Certain chapters which were obviously written out of order simply because he wanted to at the time or because a particular idea, memory or reminder started a train of thought that needed to be put down, are like little essays in themselves; my obvious aim has been to keep these in chronological order (although with overlaps and digressions this was quite difficult!), to use Vernon's own words entirely, but avoid the frequent repetition without destroying the sense and not be too ruthless with an old man's musings which add so much to the character study and personality portrait of the subject.

Apart from certain references to his (much) later life, almost all Vernon's writing goes no further than his father's death. For him, that was the end of an era of his life he was ever reluctant to let go. Those Edwardian memories, his reverence for women in all walks of life, his preoccupation with life 'downstairs' and the servant maids personified by Marie, stayed with him, frequently being resurrected in his painting just as anything that becomes a major influence in the life of an artist intrudes into his art. He always felt that these "utterly underrated hardworking, humble girls — now gone forever — were the prop of society". He said once that although no stately homes could have existed without them, no lady could have been beautifully dressed, no real home life, including meals, could have existed or allowed any leisure to the better off family, no honour had been given them until that modern television show — 'Upstairs — Downstairs'.

My anthology, therefore, falls into two parts. The first, though pulled together through a collection of writings, is all his own, and to him the important part. The second is a combination of my own knowledge and research and the memories of others. Together we may, once and for all, be able to dispel the distorted image of a painter of pretty swans and flying birds!

Chapter One
EARLIEST MEMORIES

I was born to be an artist — the answer to my father's personal desire! He, Albert Ward, an antiquarian, Irish, colourful, talented, a fine pianist and a well-educated man, was the son of James Isaac Ward from Cork in Ireland, also an antiquarian. Isaac Ward, from earning a living as a factory hand at the age of fourteen, by his own efforts became an expert on 17th century Dutch painting. Before he died in poverty, caused by extravagant living, drink and giving up his dealing in Old Masters to follow a new love — fatally as it turned out — of buying the works of the French Impressionists, he was laughed at, neglected his business and tried to find oblivion in drink.

In this he was completely successful: the Impressionist paintings became pink elephants and other visions of a drug and drink sodden world. I should like to pay tribute to this brave, sad man who rose from nothing, then sank to the pauper's infirmary, dying there one night after saying good-bye to my father and thanking him for all he had done.

My father's bright future as a gentleman of leisure was thus brought to an abrupt halt. There were a few years of odd jobs playing dance music (he had a small orchestra), then the meeting with my mother at a dance hall in Hampstead where now the Royal Free Hospital rears its massive concrete structure dwarfing the houses of Victorian humbleness. One of these was my home where, on a bright October morning, I emerged quietly from my mother's womb. The doctor, elegant in silk top hat and black frock-coat, was just in time to prevent me from hauling myself back by the umbilical cord. . . I knew by intuition that my life was going to be difficult, that I would never say "boo" to a goose and that my fantastic ignorance of life (perhaps ignoring would be a better term) would be my undoing. So it proved to be after many happy years, years of love from my strong, resolute mother and my talented, gay and scholarly father.

I loved my father with the passion of a woman and it was reciprocated completely. There was nothing I would not do to please him — I even tried to play the piano which was a complete mystery and a dreadful penance at my tender age. I could only make sense of drawing and painting; this was so natural to me that I never remember being taught to mix colours or how to apply them. However, later I learned the deeper joys of painting the infinite variety of tones and shades of colour made by mixing white with just one colour.

By the time my father was putting up purple painted boards over his picture shop windows (one of which contained a large colour reproduction of King Edward, 'good old Teddy' as the King was affectionately termed in those far off Edwardian days) and I was taken out of my girls' clothes and now wore sailor suits of blue jersey and round wide hats with upturned brims and 'H.M.S. Belleraphon' in white letters on the wide, blue ribbons, I was completely immersed in art and artists and under instruction from the many and varied artists who came to my father's shop.

Vernon's great-grandfather.

Isaac James Ward, Vernon's grandfather.

Vernon's grandmother with his father.

Albert Ward, Vernon's father, at his easel, c.1920.

Albert Ward's antique shop in Hampstead.

Mary Ward, Vernon's mother.

Albert Ward with his wife Mary and children, Kyrle, Eric and Vernon.

Chapter Two
AT OUR SHOP

The building where I was born is still there although my father's antique shop is now a well known grocery store.

One very early memory I have is of the Edwardian gentlemen or their maids who were sent to us with photographs of the then so recent Boer War. The relief of Ladysmith and of Mafeking were still talked about; the widows went about in widows' weeds, the boys wore black armbands, some little girls wore black drawers and so did many of the ladies. Death was an all absorbing topic as it is today but the display of death then was prodigious. Why? I cannot imagine. The grief embarrassed me since my shyness was, as I continue to mention, pathological in its awful effect on my nature.

So, I would run into my father's shop at a very early age. If there was a customer talking I would slink past quietly or wait outside watching until the coast was clear. Very soon I was taught to call ''Right'' as the bell clanged when I opened the door which saved my father coming to the door from a little curtained-off parlour. Inside the shop were the most fascinating articles, some of which now would be very valuable. My father's pride was his honesty, in fact he was too honest if that can be, for he was unmercifully treated, just as I was to be after his death in 1926. He opened the shop about eight o'clock and closed when his work was done; nobody hurried in those days, it was a standard of life for the lower middle class into which I was born to expect very little from life and to work all hours of the day to achieve that little.

All the while I eagerly sought the side of my father. I see him now after all these strange years — handsome, smiling, bending over a picture, cleaning it — he had 'Restoration of Old Masters a Speciality' printed on a large white card underneath a stern faced Victorian portrait, one side of which was cleaned, the other half grimy and cracked with a small hole in it. Other cards advertised framing of all kinds, valuable china neatly riveted, glass cut while you wait, mirrors resilvered, furniture repaired and valuations of all objets d'art, distance no object. On

Thursdays, half day in Hampstead, he went to the sales and with his pathetically limited purse, he bought shrewdly, mainly at Willis's Rooms, opposite Christie's. Later I went with him, school permitting, and enlarged my knowledge of artists not generally known to the average public.

Our pitiable profits meant a sort of genteel poverty while his clients bought lovely prints by Bartolotzzi, mezzotints and engravings. Many were bought by a charming elderly lady who lived in a mansion block and whose Bartolotzzi and Cipriani engravings were to be destined for the Victoria and Albert Museum. The Museum authorities, experts in the most valuable and popular type of works, would be invited to tea with this distinguished lady and I often delivered the prints. She lost her only beloved son in the Boer War, a very handsome Captain, and how well I remember her graceful charm and her deep black mourning, especially the large black hat.

I heard and learned so much behind that curtain and it was all honest and most respectable. There was no slang, no swearing and no bad talk; that was just for the drunks outside the pubs on a Saturday night. I had a boyhood friend whose father kept a very respectable inn where I spent many evenings in the holidays actually serving behind the bar which was legal as long as I did not personally take the money. I used to help cut up the new bread into squares served with cheddar cheese which lay on the counters of both public and saloon bars and which was FREE as long as one bought a drink of beer, price one penny or twopence. And the customer could eat as much as he liked, wholesome bread and cheese, not salted as so many comestibles are today so that one gets a satisfactory thirst.

Barmaids, while I am still digressing, were buxom and very attractive in figure. Oh, that hour-glass figure, that piled up hair, that elegant back that was reflected in the mirrors behind her reminding one of Édouard Manet's famous painting 'The Barmaid' whose reflection is so hopelessly wrong — poetic licence! A woman, as she is today, knows exactly how she looks from the back. In Edwardian days the bosom and the rear part were so much more exciting than they are today — plus ça change.

Back to the shop. Behind the curtain was, as I have said, a little parlour. Meals were snatched there during the day but after closing time (which could be eight o'clock or even ten) meals were served by Marie upstairs. Behind the parlour was a little greenhouse, glassed over, and used most of the time by an artist, one George Fox, a former Royal Academy student whom I watched with growing admiration. He looked exactly like Charles Dickens and he loved the latter's books as much as my father who would read out relevant passages to him and, as father rather fancied himself as a dramatic actor, would 'act out' the scene that George Fox would be painting.

He was the dearest, kindest, most generous old Victorian artist I ever met, and I met many. He encouraged me to draw, in charcoal, by the Victorian method called 'stippling' — picking out the lights or reducing the shade with bits of new bread kneaded to a point. (Putty rubber was not invented then.) Linseed oil and turpentine were kept in bottles on a shelf facing the light to get rid of the inevitable browning effect. The colours were wonderful, mostly German like the frames. Half England was pro-German so why they went to war against England always baffled me; father understood it better after a visit to Leipzig where he saw the

'An elegant arrival'.   Reproduced by courtesy of *W.R. Royle Ltd.*

Kaiser review his spike-helmeted troops: rows upon rows of the German Army, with the officers in their long coats, polished boots and, in some cases, corsets to keep their figures upright. There are plenty of photographs of these fine troops who endured the four and a half years of Hell as well as the French and British who faced them.

My father hurried back to England and said, "There is going to be a war." Speaking fluent German since he finished his education in Nuevied on the Rhine, no doubt, I assumed, gave him a secret knowledge. No one listened, of course, so when on August 4th, 1914, the morning papers proclaimed in huge headlines WAR DECLARED, poor father did no business for months. All our savings went, so too did the wonderful craftsmen he employed — French polishers, furniture makers, gilder/repairers of china, upholsterers, all seven-year apprentice men who scorned the shoddy rubbish that started to creep into the antique business. I once saw the word MARGARINE burned in the back of a so-called walnut veneered chest of drawers. I wonder what Arthur Negus would say!!

"...a Goddess stood there..."

16

I have omitted any description of myself in these early years but I must now declare that I was unbelievably shy, very nervous, timid and a very tiny boy appropriately nicknamed Tich. I hated being called Tich but was too shy and timid to ask for my real name which seemed elegant and unusual, so Tich it was for many years — except of course, at my charming, sheltered, Miss Slipper's Academy for young ladies.

In 1910 a great event came to Hampstead Heath in the form of a Kinema, a moving picture house, called the Hampstead Picture Playhouse. Proudly it reared its white stone façade, a stone's throw from my father's shops for he had prospered a little by then and taken two premises. The shops are still there and so is the cinema.

In that early cinema opposite my father's shop I saw a film of one of Scott's expeditions, mainly lantern slides and described by a member of his team. I was probably seven or eight years old, eagerly helping my father in his business, so proud to be entrusted to take out the brown paper wrapped prints or photographs he had framed. "Never go round to the tradesmen's entrance my boy, our business is an artistic one."

I recall the gaslit streets, warm bright houses, my first ring of a well polished bell. With beating heart I waited; the door opened and a Goddess stood there, tall, commanding in immaculate cap and streamers, high starched collar, frilled shoulder straps and starched bib. She waited silently, the bright hall framing her, while I licked my dry lips and gathered my flagging courage. I heard my voice, "I am from Mr. Ward at the picture shop. Will you please take this picture to Mr. and Mrs. — I am to wait for an answer."

The Goddess pondered; there was a pause while the magic words "picture shop" sank in. Her voice, musical, grave, correct, said, "You had better come in." I took off my cap and entered; the world outside was shut out. I handed her the parcel carefully and the white envelope containing the bill — the money so badly needed. "Will I get it?" I wondered.

"Wait here". The Goddess took the parcel, turned and walked majestically down the long hall, her rear even more enchanting. A beautiful fluttering pair of streamers floated from her white lace cap; her erect and shapely back was criss-crossed by the white linen straps holding her waistband tied in a splendid bow of starched, gleaming virginal white. This unearthly creature would never sit down or otherwise crush that beautiful bow.

She paused at a door, knocked quietly but with authority and entered. The sound of voices followed, then a hush... a few words from the Goddess... I waited with beating heart, cap in hand, while the grandfather clock ticked timelessly and remotely on... if only my heart would keep still... There was seven shillings and sixpence at stake and, above all, my triumph at helping to bring money to the father I worshipped. I can see him to this day, his beloved face so handsome with those laughing brown eyes and the lock of dark hair falling across a wide, generous forehead.

The pause was getting unbearable. I looked at the large engraving of Queen Victoria with her beloved Albert — he was nearly as handsome as my father. A beautiful barometer hung opposite and I remember curtains hanging a few yards down the hall under the peculiar white-green light coming from the gaslight under a white globe. The grandfather clock cleared its throat and chimed half past eight. I crept a few feet towards the curtains, every sense as alert as a redskin in one of Buffalo Bill's little weeklies that I used to read with such breathless attention.

Still the clock ticked on and my heart hammered away. Were they finding something wrong with my father's framing, I wondered, I could hear no voices from behind the thick, dark brown door. I dared not be caught listening by the white capped Goddess and crept back to the spot where she had told me to wait. In any case there might have been, behind a green baize door, another lesser Goddess in not quite such a glamorous apron but intimidating to me, none the less.

Suddenly the door opened and the parlourmaid, my Goddess, reappeared. I felt again the awe she had inspired in me as she came towards me gleaming in the gaslight.

"Mrs. — is very pleased with the framing; here is the money."

My heart leapt as I took the envelope feeling the money inside.

"Thank you," I said, then, as she opened the door and I stepped out into the night air, she suddenly unbent and became human.

"This is for you Tom." She held out twopence.

"Oh, thank you," I said taking the money. My heart sang as I walked and skipped down Pond Street; into the warm lighted shop I went, ring went the bell and I called out "Right." We always called out "Right" so that no one need think it was a customer.

"Here's the money Dad and Mrs. — was very pleased with the way you framed her photograph." I see now, after sixty years, my father's warm, smiling face as he took the envelope I handed him.

I loved to help in the shop and with the delivery and collection of pictures to be framed, cleaned and restored. I remember my father gilding frames after leaving them in "oils" overnight, the five shilling books of gold leaf, the little palette with the paper shield, the knife to cut the gold leaf which was blown out carefully from the little tissue paper leaves that enclosed each wafer thin leaf of gold. The slightest draught caused by anyone entering the workshop sent the incredibly thin leaf soaring up to the ceiling where the hot air kept it fluttering, a glittering butterfly. I remember my father's exasperation, his "suffer fools gladly" muttered imprecation as he followed the fluttering gold leaf, finally to catch it as it slowly sank into the little palette covered with chamois leather. This was when the outbreak of war in August 1914 caused him reluctantly to dismiss old Wilson who did all the gilding and forced him to go back to the bench himself.

Returning to what now seems a warm, secure golden age, I remember my father's love of artists and the bohemian life they often led. It was as true then as today that the real artist is outside the steady discipline of the everyday working existence which is the lot of everyman. George Fox was trained in the Academy Schools; a figure artist of no great merit but with a heart of gold and the heart of a child. Living gaily as so many painters did from day to day, he begun to owe his landlady several weeks' rent. His worry over this brought on a severe nervous breakdown and, as I know only too well, the inability to paint. He lived at Croydon and thought nothing of walking to Hampstead to enjoy Long's Tea Rooms, a quite fashionable thing to do for an outing during the summer, and he

18

went one day to my father's shop and, in desperation, asked if he, my father, would buy a few odd stretchers he had by him. My father's instant sympathetic reaction and my mother providing him with a good hot meal, resulted in George Fox coming to work — painting pictures of scenes from Charles Dickens, a speciality of this old artist. Broken in health, he found in the picture shop in Hampstead a haven, where for ten shillings a day and the feeling of once more belonging to a family, he became part of our existence. He helped to put figures in old canvases bought cheaply by my father at odd sales, in the meantime at my father's instigation and with his encouragement, continuing to paint well-known episodes from the more popular works of Charles Dickens.

It was in this atmosphere that I spent my early childhood. As I grew up I knew the sound of the shop bell, saw the two easels, my father's always with some old master painting, usually Dutch, of landscape, flowers or a portrait, or later pictures of other schools, and that of George Fox behind my father's, both in a tiny space no more that 12ft. by 6ft. The atmosphere was pervaded with the pungent smells of oil colour, turpentine, methylated spirit and the thick tobacco smoke from Mr. Fox's terrible pipe in which he seemed to find a great solace and renewal of his flagging strength. I realise now although it never occurred to me at the time how difficult it must have been to work under those conditions but, later, I too was fitted into this crowded space, my tiny five year old figure sitting on a stool and drawing a plaster cast of a head using the aforementioned charcoal with bits of bread.

Every spare minute I was either watching Mr. Fox painting or trying to paint myself. When my father was out at the sales or in his workshop, I was allowed to use his easel and given a coloured picture postcard to copy on a little canvas board. Thus encouraged and supervised, I painted many copies of postcards and other pictures; I began to grow quite proficient and later sold some of my copies for two shillings and sixpence until my father found out and I was forbidden ever to become tainted with the lure of money. I remember the feeling of shame at displeasing my beloved father and I resolved to do everything he required of me. He was insistent that I drew and redrew the plaster heads and although I found it tedious work, I toiled away at it using every spare hour from school and in the holidays.

I was not in very good health, highly strung, extremely nervous and abnormally shy. I worked so hard that I began to have minor breakdowns and my mother had words with father accusing him of driving me too hard — which was only too true, although I needed no driving.

I look back and see my happy, correct, striving innocent self, talented, a born artist, born to every privilege that an artistic environment could offer. So many artists assisted me in my work, perhaps knowing that it would please my father but more likely simply responding to the generous impulses of those struggling themselves but still ready to encourage a small boy to paint and never to think of doing anything else.

Knowing how many good artists lived and died in poverty, my mother grew apprehensive at my entering into this precarious way of life. I was too shy, too timid and, above all, far too sensitive to make my way into the world of the artist — she saw no romance in starving in a garret wearing a big floppy black bow and having a careless attitude to all practical aspects of life. She had many an altercation over me, the only words my parents ever had between them for they had a deep love for each other and were only concerned for my future.

"Don't make the boy mercenary" was my father's continual cry and my mother would retort "Look at so-and-so... ending their lives with nothing, living on charity or a daughter or the kindness of those who had only known the hard grind of business and the humdrum world."

As I grew older I was forced to realise that behind the glamour of the artist — and there is glamour aided and abetted by plays, stories and the life histories of well-known artists, there was a very different aspect to such a life. There is melancholy, and appalling strain getting worse as success comes, for if climbing the ladder is difficult and utterly demanding, it is nothing to staying on top once an artist has got there.

"We arrived to find a crowd of children..."

Chapter Three
KINDERGARTEN YEARS

The ceremony of being 'breeched' took place when I was about five years old, a ritual in most Edwardian families where there were male children. Before this, little boys were dressed as girls and wore their hair long; many a fond mama shed a few tears when her son's long curls were cut off and his female attire was replaced by a boy's sailor suit — dark blue for winter and white for summer.

I remember crying miserably as my mother, with Marie standing by, took off my dress, my wide blue (for a boy) sash, my cambric petticoats and lace edged drawers, my liberty bodice and long vest. I stood naked and in tears for I sensed the wind of change and didn't like it. Other boys did; to them it meant they could climb trees, use catapults (secretly!), shin over walls for a dare and go 'scrumping.' In my almost pathological shyness I felt I was being lured into a world I feared but the breeching went on — I remember my mother saying kindly as she put me into a pair of knickerbockers and a jersey that did up on the left shoulder with three black buttons, "Look, you've got pockets now," but her soothing voice only added to my secret fears. I didn't want pockets. I wanted the little green purse that hung round my neck and contained a child's treasures mainly, I remember, a penny.

I got over the loss of my clothes when my first sailor suit arrived. White was for summer, blue serge for winter; there was a lanyard with a whistle attached that went into a breast pocket, a striped collar, a wide straw hat with turned up brim and navy-blue ribbon around the crown sporting the name of a famous ship. Yes, the pockets were exciting and were soon filled with bits of elastic, string, marbles, a small toy — all the clutter that a small boy accumulates.

Vernon dressed as a girl.

Then came the first day of going to a Kindergarten School — how can I possibly describe the happiness of that school? Every day seems in retrospect a golden dream. The school was actually a Young Ladies' Academy in a large private house about ten minutes walk from my home. The Principal, a tall, austere, grey-haired and very formidable lady ran the school for girls of all ages, indeed many finished their education there except for the customary period in France or Switzerland to learn European languages, but little boys were accepted under approved circumstances. Under Miss Slipper and her younger sister, Miss Helen, who took charge of the very young assisted by a very pretty dark-haired French woman, I soon forgot my sexual metamorphosis.

Our maid, Marie, took me to school, and we arrived to find quite a crowd of children, girls of all ages, and nursemaids (some with prams for baby's airing), all waiting for the hour of nine. Then the doors opened and the pupils trooped up the beautifully hearthstoned white steps and into a long large passage.

On each side of the passage ran a mahogany shelf lined with hooks from which hung a row of scarlet canvas bags containing plimsolls for which we exchanged our boots — shoes were rare in those days. A mistress helped me to change my boots for the plimsolls already provided and hats were placed on a shelf above the hooks. All this changing and hanging up of hats and coats was conducted in silence except for a few whispered instructions, then the main door was opened and in we went. I found myself in a large room that was converted into an even larger one by a second room that had folded partitions on each side of two central pillars.

Two huge mahogany tables ran down the centre and forms lined these tables for the pupils. There were no desks.

There was a roll-call and we all stood to attention. Then Morning Prayers were said, the children dutifully chanting them. Miss Helen sat at a piano by the door and played a hymn followed by a simple song. I remember the first one so clearly, all about a dandelion that had somehow strayed into a garden bed where none of the other flowers would have anything to do with it. So there was class even among the flowers!

Before going further I feel I should add here that my father was very much the educated Edwardian gentleman. His antique shop was full of beautiful things from which I gained my early appreciation of china, Sèvres, Crown Derby, Rockingham, etc., as well as the paintings he dealt in. He was an expert on the 17th Century Dutch School in which he specialised. Nevertheless, when he approached Miss Slipper with a view to my becoming a pupil at her academy, he met with a decisive "No". Miss S. calmly told him that she did not take children of tradesmen!

Controlling himself with a mighty effort for my father was quick-tempered over such blatant snobbery, he persuaded her that he sold objects of great beauty — in themselves an education. Such reasoning, plus the fact that he read Greek and spoke German and French fluently, won the day. No doubt his handsome face and figure helped overcome these rigid principles and so I entered Heaven — to be banished once more when I was too old because I was a boy.

Strangely, I felt instantly at home in this school. I hated noise and was often in ailing health with headaches and earache, so the quiet obedience expected (and insisted upon!) from every middle-class child was one reason that these years were the happiest I was ever to know. I look back with gratitude that I was born in such an era when England was great and powerful and when Law and Order prevailed. When our maid, Marie, said that she "knew her place" she said it with pride. Rightly or wrongly, I was taught this Edwardian fact and in the Kindergarten, it was the very air we breathed.

After prayers and the singing the youngest children climbed up the stairs to a large room at the back of the house where Miss Stone, a tall angular woman who always dressed in brown, took us in charge. We played with square bricks with large capital letters on the sides making simple words such as CAT, DOG, etc., learning to spell while comparing CAT (or whatever) with a picture of a cat or other animal or object. It was very effective but it also began to bore me; in exasperation Miss Stone finally sent me down to the main room to tell the formidable Miss Slipper that I was disobedient.

I knocked at the door and at the words, "Come in," I entered, trembling.

I beheld two long rows of bent heads — all girls. No one looked up; there was utter silence. The the Principal adjusted her pince-nez and said: "Come here child."

I crept along the rows of studious heads with their varying hair styles and colouring and stood downcast before the dreaded Presence. She listened to my explanation, then signed to a tall, dark-haired girl, Christine C., who instantly got up (how she saw the signal, I never knew). Miss Slipper said, "Take this child Christine and look after him."

An Edwardian schoolgirl.

So, I found myself sitting next to this splendid girl for the rest of the day. I have to confess I found this experience enchanting. Christine, I found out later, was the Head Girl; she wore a white blouse and a dark blue serge skirt and she found me an exercise book to copy words into. I deliberately made myself a nuisance upstairs to be sent downstairs as a punishment and, to my joy, was told to sit next to Christine every day.

So the days passed into weeks and into terms. Never was I so happy. I was even awarded a prize for deportment (I have it today), a book illustrated by Arthur Rackham — *Gulliver's Travels*. Winter, Spring, Autumn, I loved those days; I was never clever but this method of teaching suited me perfectly. I learned everything of value in those early years, those golden years when a child observes much more than parents or grown-ups ever realise.

In those days a great reticence existed regarding such simple necessities as leaving the room. No child ever got down from the table whether at home or at school without first asking permission, ever slouched in a chair or put hands in pockets. Good manners were prized above all things; boys were taught to revere girls and women, no matter what class, a woman was different and that was that — even if boys did sometimes pull the girls' pigtails!

So when I wished to 'leave the room' at school, that is to go to the lavatory, I put up my hand. No one ever looked up, the bent heads remained studiously working. Miss Slipper, who saw everything from her vantage point at the head of the table, would enquire what I wanted. "Please Miss, may I leave the room?"

"If the marker is there you may."

Still no one stirred. The "marker" was the lid of a wooden pencil box and I remember that it had faded flowers on it. I would rise up and quietly cross over to the marble mantelpiece, feel for the marker as I was not tall enough to see if it was there and finding it, I took it and left the room. Upstairs was the loo, a grand affair completely enclosed in dark mahogany. On lifting the massive lid there was disclosed a bowl covered with blue designs; a small hole at the side revealed a handle. When this was pulled a metal lid at the bottom of the bowl dropped down and at the same time a flood of water gushed out. It was all very exciting. Thrilling, too, was the great adventure that came next. No one in Edwardian days was ever to be seen leaving the lavatory, it was simply "not done." So there was much peering through a half-opened door and only when one was completely sure that nobody was in sight did one creep out, marker in hand, to open the main door carefully, close it gently, cross by the rows of bent, studious heads, replace the marker and slide back into one's place as if nothing had happened.

Any Edwardians who may be reading this will remember only too vividly the truth of what I have described. When lessons were over, at mid-day and at 4 o'clock, we changed our plimsolls for outdoor boots, put on our coats and hats and with courteous good-byes, the girls giving a little curtsey to Miss Slipper and Miss Helen, we went out into the air where nursemaids or maids were awaiting their charges. It was all very decorous, a part of life that has vanished for ever with words like 'deportment' and 'demure' and phrases such as "Do not fidget", "Never slouch", "Hands out of pockets", "No running or shouting". In my Kindergarten there was complete obedience; one look of displeasure from any of

"...to my joy, was told to sit next to Christine every day."

The daisy chain.

26

the mistresses was quite sufficient to quell any high spirits.

There was no punishment, for it was never needed. The streets were safe, the policeman on the beat was a friend. The lamplighter went on his way, his magic pole causing the gas lamps to spring into life. I went back happily, to a home where my mother awaited me and all was well — in those peaceful, happy Kindergarten years.

One other charming custom was the end of the term at Christmas. On the last morning we all brought our Christmas cards, the names of the recipients written or printed on the envelopes, and handed them to Miss Helen to put in a pillowcase. Of course, after prayers, we sang all the well-known carols and at about 11 o'clock we all had large plates of biscuits. I particularly remember these with animal pictures in brown or white icing.

Then the pillowcase of Christmas cards was emptied on the table and thoroughly mixed. The excitement was intense. We sat around and the formidable Miss Slipper, this time benign and indulgent (she really was much beloved), called out the names as, one by one, she picked out a card. We came forward to receive them, the girls curtseying and the little boys shyly thanking the Principal with a stiff little bow.

Of course the mistresses had a special pile of cards, we all gave them one, and for once there was noise, the noise of happy children at ease and showing the exchange of friendship that this splendid school instilled into all who had the good fortune to have such a perfect education. I say perfect because it was intelligent, stressing good behaviour and good manners above everything else.

What I learned there has remained with me all my life. Cleanliness, in mind as well as body, was next to Godliness and we believed it. The immaculate dress of the Principal and staff, the long skirts touching the ground, the high-boned lace necks of their blouses, the quiet colours, the impeccable behaviour, the absence of bullying or any form of aggression fills me with gratitude for my father's persistence in getting me into such an establishment.

I recently walked over the Heath between the Hampstead Ponds and retraced my steps, now severely limited by arthritis, and came to the corner house where my school was. There was the house in good repair. The very name had been retained and I stood at the foot of the stone steps. The road was littered with the usual assortment of garageless cars.

I saw in memory the group of nannies and maids awaiting the opening at nine o'clock of a Kindergarten and Young Ladies' Academy. The road was deserted then, no noise, no aircraft droning overhead, perhaps just a butcher's cart with its sprightly horse trotting past. Life is change; it has to be. We are all destined to grow up and away into our Destiny. When I was forced to leave having reached the age limit (even childhood has its limits), I went to the complete reverse of such schooling. It was in 1913.

Where are they now, all those upright, in every way, Edwardian ladies? Where are those nannies and maids? Why is childhood so innocent and so capable of finding happiness in a toy, a doll, a 'pretend' world?

It is full of ghosts, that road where I had my first schooling, ghosts that charm. They do not frighten because there was no fear. For me, the son of a highly educated father and a beautiful mother whose marriage was a complete success, there was security and happiness and, above all, innocence in a home where family life was well ordered. Oh, for that Edwardian era, vanished now for ever.

. . . .

Editor's note: Under the heading of 'Betrayal' Vernon Ward has written of an incident which must have occurred during the period of Kindergarten years, the years following breeching and at Kindergarten School. Obviously it had a profound effect on his hypersensitive nature, not soon to be tucked away in the subconscious but haunting him, every detail printed clearly on his conscious memory, for the rest of his life.

. . . .

In my youth I suffered from headaches, earache and toothache; the shrill cries of exuberant children put my nerves on edge and I tended naturally towards quieter and more reflective occupations.

It was full summer or so it seems looking back on that long summer of Edwardian childhood and I had wandered out on to the nearby Hampstead Heath, the 'first heath' as it was called. The willows, now grown old like myself, drooped in yellowy fringed beauty making this corner of the Heath a natural playground. Nannies sat upon seats by large blue prams with fringed canvas hoods to keep the sun off the babies, the nannies themselves armed against the deadly sun's rays by bonnets and brown alpaca uniforms over which an ample white bibbed apron gleamed spotlessly. No doubt they gossiped together about their charges and the ladies they served.

In the long green grass sat a little circle of five or six small girls all dressed in white cotton frocks, their hair tied with white or pink ribbon — no girls ever went about without their hair-ribbon. This white-dressed feminine circle sat demurely intent on making daisy chains. A little heap of these sweet dainty flowers lay in the centre; they grew abundantly in the long grass and in consequence had good long stalks to support their white fringed golden heads.

I used to stand, an outcast, outside this hallowed circle morning after sunny morning while they, the demure ones, complete in their encircled strength, dolls at sides, ornate white shady hats over serious young heads, bent over this entirely female occupation. One day, I suppose it would be after I was breeched which of course put me hopelessly outside the circle, perhaps about 1909, I stood looking on at a respectful distance. The eldest girl, herself about four years old, looked up and said coldly, "Well, Boy," the word 'Boy' as if it were a bad smell — "what do you want?"

Overcoming my dreadful shyness, I blurted out — "I was... er... I was... er..." I took the plunge, "I wish I could make daisy chains."

There was a surprised silence, small fingers ceased plaiting daisies, even the dark brown bumbling bees ceased to bumble and listened, wings folded.

A Boy, one of the loathsome tribe of snaps and snails and puppy dogs' tails, wanted to learn how to make daisy chains! I blushed and stood silent while the young considered this unbelievable request. Was it that latent instinct one day to love the opposite tribe that made a whispered consultation? Fair-haired and dark-haired heads were put together and I waited. At last came the verdict, ''Very well, Boy, we will teach you.''

I sat down humbly in the space indicated, was given a few long-stalked daisies, and I felt soft hands guiding my clumsy fingers in my first lesson in making the enchanting daisy chains.

Thereafter I would seek them out and sit with them in sunlit peace, my head shaded from the dreaded sunshine by a large straw hat with 'H.M.S. Belleraphon' in gold letters on its blue ribbon. I did not join in the talk being a 'foreigner' but I was content, my loneliness banished.

And then came a group of boys! They stared at me — a boy making daisy chains. Yah, a cissy!! I had no idea what a cissy was but knew I was breaking a boys' code. I jumped up furious, ''I'm not, I'm not,'' I yelled and ran after the jeering mob. I remember I had to prove this by climbing a willow tree and swinging far out on a branch, letting go and dropping to the ground with a thud that made my head ache.

After that I was cut dead by the girls. I had 'quit' so I was out, never again to experience that summer peace, the gentle creativeness of the enchanted daisy chain. The first betrayal? The child psychiatrist was not invented in those uncomplicated days. I had no sisters, little girls were 'sugar and spice and all things nice'; they had been kind but I was proved to be a typical example of a 'snap and snail' boy, utterly contemptible, and small white clad figures with bowed heads under dark ringlets of sausage curls or pigtails hanging down and tied with pink bows never looked up again as I stood — outside for ever, the outsider, one of the other tribe... For in those far off days, vanished for ever, a girl was indeed a girl; as she grew she became apart from little boys, a separate bedroom, mysterious clothes and equally baffling ailments.

. . . .

A very few years later, as a boy of about seven years old, I received another severe shock. I had been taught to revere and respect womanhood, to strike a woman was the act of a cad and for a boy to hit a girl brought a very severe thrashing from father, mother or elder brother.

An Edwardian woman was really a grand sight, wasp-waisted, bell-skirted with many petticoats, high-boned blouse necks of lace and lace frilled jabots frothing down over swelling bosoms, upholstered bosoms with sometimes a watch pinned on her breast or pince-nez attached to a little silver case that was also pinned to her blouse and could be drawn out, the safety wire emerging with a zizzing noise that fascinated me. At her slim waist, made to look even more tiny by the leg-of-mutton sleeves, she sometimes wore the châtelaine, a lovely jangling affair of objects dangling on silver chains, the indispensable button hook (every woman had to have one to button her boots and gloves), a tiny silver pencil, the inevitable phial of smelling salts, a key or two and so on. Hair was piled high over matching pads, a tiresome chore often needing a tiny pair of hair tongs heated over a little spirit flame on the dressing table.

How completely different was the Edwardian woman. The 'new' woman was emerging but slowly; with tremendous daring she mounted her bicycle and with her male escort in frogged tight-fitting cycling clothes, went off on Sundays. My father was an ardent cyclist and persuaded my mother to try it; many delightful Sundays they had with the Club, passing the carriages clip-clopping back from Church, the occupants staring at these gay young men and women liberating themselves from the oppressive Sundays of Edwardian England. One day I wandered up to the Spaniards Road where, by a pond, was a sort of Speakers' Corner. Anyone had the right to speak on any subject and the small crowd would listen in good humoured tolerance as the British always did. I listened to a woman putting forward the woman's point of view. They had a part to play in public life, she urged. I do not remember much of her speech but the mood of the men changed; two or three brawny 'gentlemen' got hold of her and dragged her, protesting, to the pond and threw her in . . . I stared aghast! It was not a deep pond and was really for horses and carts to wade through to cool the horses in summer so I was not actually alarmed for her safety. It was the sight of a well-dressed woman scrambling to her feet, her wide brimmed hat streaming water, her long skirts clinging to her legs, dragging herself out amid the jeers and cat-calls of the men that brought my first sense of shame into my consciousness. My father always declared himself to be a feminist and pro-suffrage for women; he always spoke up for women's rights and had always brought me up to listen to any alternative points of view. Now here, before my horrified gaze, I saw a decent, well-dressed woman, unaided and alone, having to struggle out of the white stone pond where I sailed my boats in the summer days of Edwardian England. I ran away from this desecration of all I held so perfect, ran to my father, bursting into the picture shop at the corner of Pond Street, and poured out my story in tearful gasps. I never forgot it, never can. There is a strange love-hate relationship between man and woman, it persists as if Adam cannot forgive Eve for his own weakness.

. . . .

Chapter Four
FURTHER EDWARDIAN REMINISCENCES

Editor's note: Over and over again in the writings scattered amongst Vernon's papers, in essays perhaps one day to have been made into a book or collection, in letters written but never posted or just as thoughts on scraps of paper, his Edwardian childhood resurrects itself. It seems appropriate here to quote a few more extracts (somewhat abbreviated for, as aforesaid, Vernon was a master of both repetition and digression), not only to provide further insight into his complex character but to add to the general domestic history of the Edwardian era when, as Vernon would have us believe, the sun always shone and there was love and laughter, security and peace. Certainly there was up to the time of the dreaded 'breeching'. . .

After I had been breeched — changed into a boy — I became aware of my isolation. My shyness increased and I could not accept the world of a boy with its greater robustness, noise and added freedom. It seemed then, as I look back, a world full of nameless fears. I began to withdraw into my inner self and my nervousness grew into a sort of protective shell. A new and extremely sensitive creature, half boy and half girl, began to emerge with a consequent increase in childish aches and pains.

A mysterious earache of great severity began to afflict me with odd headaches so that I had to lie down more often; this was followed by nervous twitchings of the head similar to those of the Emperor Claudius. My 'withdrawal', my fear of a new personality resulting from the loss of my girls' clothes and, with them, the protected existence peculiar to girls of Edwardian times, became a barrier to the freedom that most boys longed for. The quiet restraints imposed on the female of the species, the very restrictions of their sex which I, instinctively or intuitively, felt to be a safe harbour, were abhorrent to the average healthy boy. In those far off days, the psychiatrist was scarcely known; doctors diagnosed 'growing pains'. There was not the reliance on drugs that there is today, perhaps some iron jelloids for suspected anaemia but no pampering, no nonsense such as recognising that some children were more sensitive than others and needed a more cautious approach in training.

The Edwardian child was to be seen and not heard. The incredible liberty of the almost precocious child of the 'seventies was very firmly put down. Obedience was enforced by the cane in the home and at school; in the poorer homes the father unbuckled his thick leather belt and thrashed his son with it, while the girls felt the cane on their thighs, skirts lifted. Thus were the first principles taught — to obey, to sit still, to go to bed at the appointed time. Even my enlightened parents, the kindest of people, showed no mercy at the slightest sign of disobedience. Out came the cane from the cupboard, as natural a part of life in those days as it is considered unnatural in these pampered times. The 'excesses' of the psychiatrist whose stupidity has actually created the 'problem child' had no existence in the Edwardian era when the Law was there to be obeyed. The policeman, massive with his six foot bulk, was the guardian of the Law and there were few criminals

who dared resist arrest. "It's a fair cop, Guv," was the thief's reply as he was led off to meet his destiny in the police court.

How well I remember the policemen going on duty for the night. They formed up into a line of formidable men in dark blue, helmets giving an awesome height, the silver badge gleaming like a talisman set in front. The powerful red necks encased in the thick collars of the uniform with the number on it in letters of silver metal, the whistle hung on its chain, a bulge on the hip betrayed the presence of the truncheon (one blow from which laid the law breaker flat out on the ground), and the 'bull's-eye' lantern was hooked on to the thick black leather belt.

To see the sergeant line up these guardians of the Law, give the order to follow him and see them tread, in slow, deliberate, measured steps, was like seeing the Guards formed up ready to receive the Imperial 'Old Guard' of Napoleon's invincible élite — invincible until they met the disciplined, red-coated British Army. Advancing with their cries of "Vive l'Emperor" the flower of France saw, for the first time in their victorious lives, something in that impassive, red-coated square that was not going to be intimidated. The Prussians had broken, the Austrians had fled, the Russians had retreated before these twice wounded veterans but NOT the British. So it was with the Edwardian police, unhurried, calm, impassive, the men in blue kept the Law. The magistrates upheld them; the Judges judged. The prisons were a fearsome hell where the criminal lay broken in a terrible cell in the costume of a convicted felon, the clothes stamped all over with green government arrows.

The photographs of the old prisons, the quarries where men broke up granite stones under the implacable eye of the wardens, brings a chill to the heart of the compassionate. A prison meant just that. The crank (treadmill) was there ready to smash rebellion by the sheer meaninglessness of its utter degradation.

Life in the gay 'nineties was good for the law-abiding who also had money. The word 'gay' was not perverted as it is today by sad, unhappy men who are cursed with something they do not understand but only know it is irrestistible. To feel gay was to sing and be happy. Happiness was an Edwardian sensation that died on the bloody battlefields of France and Belgium; it hung like a dish clout on the barbed wire with the clattering tin cans. It died on the days following the Armistice of 1918 when the ALL CLEAR sounded and men returned to a world 'fit for heroes'. As I felt lost in my boys' clothes, mourning my petticoats and my white dress with its pale sash, so the men who joined up so eagerly to fight the Hun felt lost and disillusioned in this strange new world so completely foreign to the one they knew and loved and left behind — for ever.

. . . .

The doctor was a family friend. Ours was a slim, handsome man always elegant in frock coat and silk hat. When I was born (and according to my mother I was no trouble) my eldest brother was so anxious for me to become a member of the family that he offered the doctor ninepence to prevent him taking me away again — he had, of course, been told that I had come in the doctor's black bag! I still have the doctor's receipt for the money, "on account", it says. There are one or

'Sitting out'.   *Reproduced by courtesy of W.R. Royle Ltd.*

two ink blots on the scrap of paper which lives with my birth certificate, both seventy-two years old.

Memory, that delicate instrument without which we are dead, plays that old sweet sad song of an entry into the world when Edward VII — Edward the Peacemaker — kept the peace. The sad, black-gowned 'widow of Windsor' slept at last, her long grief over. House parties where coloured Japanese lanterns lit up the long, green twilight of summer nights had become an exciting fashion in the 'naughty 'nineties'. White moths fluttered round the lanterns while starched maids in immaculate black and white offered claret cup on silver trays. Even a middle class family like ourselves with just one maid had claret cup with apple slices, orange quarters and grapes floating in a huge glass bowl, the claret thinned with one or two squirts of syphoned green lemonade, quite distinct from the tangy soda water that fizzed out so dangerously in inexpert hands.

One's doctor would always be invited to parties such as these as well as for a round of bridge or whist, the family doctor, who knew all about us children from the moment, stiff cuff sleeves rolled up, he had held us upside down and slapped life into us. This family friend and advisor called in sometimes to examine father's new purchases of pictures. It is a fact* that doctors were usually interested in pictures and I believe they still are for in waiting rooms in Harley Street and Wigmore Street, I have seen many fine examples of paintings, abstract as well as traditional.

It seemed that unless a serious operation was inevitable the ailments of the general public were easily dealt with. Tight lacing, according to my mother, was responsible and when she, or any other fashionably dressed woman, complained of a headache, the doctor would unhook the dress at the back, cut the stay-laces with a sharp penknife and say, "You cannot breathe, Madam." It made no difference though, for the slim waist, a deadly female weapon, was worth a deal of discomfort and no woman *ever* went without her corsets, dizzy spells or not. Besides, a lady was always armed with her smelling salts and her antikama tablets in a slim little tin case for easy carriage in her reticule; the handbag, of course,

Vernon and grandmother — "a Victorian of Victorians" — his mother and friend.

* Yes, this is very much an accepted fact today. (Ed.)

34

came much later. There was no make-up. Only 'loose' women wore rouge and powder except for ladies on the music hall stage who sang risqué songs.

Saturday night was an ordeal. Like most children we all had a Gregory powder in a spoonful of jam to take away the horrible taste. My grandmother, a Victorian of Victorians, sternly bade us swallow it and stop making a fuss. Mother later contrived to hide a Little Liver Pill in a grape and this worked fairly well. On the whole children were very healthy, the 'complex' was unknown and obedience was the word in the Edwardian family. Sex was ignored, largely unknown and never discussed, neither was the word 'loo', beloved of the ladies, as it concerned the appalling embarrassment we had over the natural functions.

''Please may I leave the room?'' was all we ever said. It was considered vulgar to be seen leaving the lavatory; we used to hide there until the coast was clear, then gently slip back into life again! Coarse talk and jokes would have been instantly punished, physically, or we were sent to bed supperless.

The doctor was always very kindly and understanding as he asked us to show him our tongues. This was the infallible approach as the tongue was the pulse. Measles, chicken-pox, whooping-cough (treatment by a long-stemmed kettle filling the room with steam was very exciting) and other childish ailments gave little anxiety, grapes and books soon restored the even tenor of family life.

It all flowed gently on. There was a considerable amount of hair lice and the Saturday baths (on Friday nights!) saw some vigorous hair washing in yellow barred, pungent Monkey Brand soap. Every home had a scurf comb. Food was plain and very pure but childish appetites were in tremendous form. Bread and cheese was a staple item even offered free in the public houses when one bought a glass of beer for one penny or two.

If Saturday nights were a penance, the highlight of the day was the 'Saturday penny', one's very own money to spend as one chose. I usually laid mine out with a sherbet dab or bag (for a ha'penny), this was a triangular bag with a tube of black liquorice to suck up the sherbet and finally be eaten. The rest went on a farthing length of black liquorice that could be torn into strips like boot laces to make it last and, finally, a farthing wafer of dark brown, rough chocolate.

The penny could be varied in its purchasing power but the penny as such was the rule even in better off families. Any more that might be given to us by visiting uncles or from any other source, had to be solemnly put in 'the box'.

. . . .

When I was a litte boy I used to collect butterflies and moths; my father encouraged it as he did most of my interests and he bought me a very fine microscope. Through this extra 'eye' I entered another world. A repellent bluebottle became a veritable Dante's inferno, with wings of marvellous structure and eyes that were of the very Devil himself. I shuddered at the terrible legs, the horrible claws, the hairs. . . I withdrew my horrified gaze! I suddenly thought — someone made it. What ghastly fiend made it? There was the awful buzz as it crashed against the window, then lay on its back kicking and spinning wildly in its death agonies. ''Oh, my God, my God,'' I breathed, for I had seen Hell.

Later I found some pieces of green cheese and put a tiny pinch on the slide.

With beating heart I adjusted the lens. A blur slowly revolved, seemingly a mighty world revolving slowly in Eternity, slowing down at my magic command.

"Oh, no . . . Oh, God, no, no, no . . ." I clung to the table. I felt sick. A terrible world of sightless creatures came into focus; my heart hammered and I desperately struggled for control, forced myself not to scream. When I looked at the slide as I withdrew it from the lens, all I saw was a tiny smear of cheese. I picked up the microscope. Evidently I was not the stuff that scientists are made of!

I turned to the wonder of my caterpillars in an old shoe box, the lid covered with butter muslin. I felt that I was God, for did I not collect the eggs and put them in my box with earth and nettle leaves or leaves from the plant I found them on? Every day I removed the lid and watched them eat the leaves, leading their own lives in their own little world. Then one day I found them looking rather odd and I knew they were dying — or were they? I saw their bodies shrivel and hang under a leaf; every day I examined them, sometimes twice a day, studying these dead things that had once been eggs, then each egg a caterpillar, now a chrysalis.

Then one day, a lovely sunny late summer morning, it happened. Not Jesus walking on the water, not the Virgin Mary appearing at Lourdes, but my very own miracle. I opened the box and stared in amazement. The bottom of the chrysalis had opened and hanging half out was a feeble, wavering thing, not repellent or evil but just hanging, apparently exhausted. No doctor stood by, no starched Marie with bowls of water and towels, no anxious father paced up and down downstairs. It was just a butterfly being born.

I watched in delight and awe. Presently it gained strength and crawled away from the dead womb upwards towards the light, crumpled, tiny and deformed with tight creased excrescences on its back. It began to unfold the packed parachute-like creased bits of crumpled material. I held my breath for surely I was witnessing God in action. After all I knew it had been a tiny egg, then a tiny caterpillar all alone with no one to tell it what to do, no one to tuck it up or comfort it, give it a sweet to suck or leave a nightlight in a saucer of water to banish the fearful shadows of a darkened bedroom. A tiny gleam of moisture appeared on the furry body, the crumpled bits went on unfolding, slowly they began to stretch, to flatten out and move wearily up and down under my very eyes. And so I watched the beautiful wings of the Red Admiral butterfly grow into their full glory, a wonderful, glorious creature with all the 'know-how' in its consciousness of what to eat, what to avoid, how to mate and how to die. Reincarnation while you wait!

I took the box to the window. The butterfly waved its wings then, all of a sudden, took off so quietly, beautifully and soundlessly, floating carelessly into the summer sunshine. I have painted many butterflies since then on wild flowers — or tried, ever striving for the impossible. After more than sixty years I remember that miracle, my eyes torn open by suffering still see the incomparable, unpaintable beauty and marvel at the extraordinary regeneration of a Red Admiral* in 1914.

. . . .

*See colour illustrations on pages 37, 40, 41 and 44.

Reproduced by courtesy of W.R. Royle Ltd.

Sometimes I sit and recall some of the Edwardian articles and customs now missing from the average, much less interesting, modern home.

The ewer — a jug for water to wash one's hands and face when arriving or staying at friends or relatives.

The 'slop' pail, often of white china with a straw wrapped handle.

The washstand, marble topped, tiled back and sides, usually tiles with pictures on them.

The brass railed bed (now fashionable again!).

The chest of drawers, the top drawer divided into two, the other three long and getting deeper until the 'bottom drawer' used by girls saving for their marriage; the trousseau was kept there in tissue paper. In the two top drawers were kept stockings or socks, gloves, handkerchiefs, a small work-basket and such private treasures as a diary, sometimes with a key for the brass clasp.

On the top of the chest of drawers there were, generally, a little swing mirror with three little drawers under for odds and ends like collar studs and a china dish for combs and hair pins. A pincushion hung on the uprights of the mirror which was usually made of mahogany or satin or pear wood, the glass usually bevelled. There would be a small china tree with branches for rings, lockets and jet ornaments to be hung on before retiring, a Bible, a brass travelling clock or one with the pendulum swinging around in a circular direction, soundless, and always under a glass dome.

A sampler worked by some little girl in needlework hung upon the much patterned wallpaper, also texts such as 'God bless this Home'. A commode stood by the bed, its two small shelves modestly enclosed by its little door, containing the usual intimate *vase de nuit*. A piece of straw carpeting was by the washstand to stand on whilst washing; in the cupboard was a hip bath and stone hot waterbottles with stoppers in the middle. The brass or copper warming pan, once so general, was rarely used. During illness a fire was burned in the grate covered with the usual iron screen. The candlestick and oil lamp or gas jet were, of course, part of the Edwardian scene.

All children wore flannel nightgowns and knelt to say prayers. Bedtime was as much of a trial as it is today but the call for a glass of water was countered by the fact that every washstand had a glass carafe with its glass on top ready for drinking. The winters were so cold that I have known the water in the jugs to be frozen.

The maid, spotless in pink, blue or lavender with cap and collar and starched cuffs, roused the children about seven-thirty. Every child had to appear at breakfast faultlessly attired, the girls in pinafores frilled over the shoulder and buttoned at the back. On every chest of drawers was a vase for the hatpins, long, very ornate affairs, and the button-hook. Without the button-hook, life was difficult.

For the man a case of razors (cut-throats) and a razor strop hung from the washstand and, of course, scissors in various sizes, some ornate in special cases. Brushes, silver or ivory backed, lay on top of the dressing table or chest of drawers.

A wardrobe with a long mirror was a usual article, satinwood, mahogany or oak, for clothes, shoes and button boots. The long boots for girls needed much buttoning with the button-hook; lacing up long boots was also quite a trial, especially as the laces had to be tied in a bow so that they hung down with some symmetry.

Luggage was the portmanteau and the wickerwork basket, top as well as bottom being used for holidays, with a strap to hold everything in place. The huge chest, brass-edged, and the leather hat box came too. The feather boa and the fan, once so generally worn, are museum pieces now and the jingling châtelaine is music long silenced along with the street cries.

Fogs were so thick then a London 'pea-souper' would last several days, deep and choking. The 'winter-warmers' were a hot potato or a tin with a live hot ember in it.

All boys and many girls wore 'blakeys' under the heels and toes of their boots and exciting sparks could be induced by striking them on the pavement. Skipping ropes for girls were as much in evidence as pinafores, and for the boys tops, marbles and cigarette card throwing against a wall. To flick it well, one wetted the end of the card which flew better that way. There was hopscotch, too, with lines chalked on the pavement or alleyway.

The motor car was so rare and so noisy that even to cling on to the back of one was a thrill. The cry of ''Whip behind, guvnor,'' was a more familiar one as the boys hung on to the back of the horse-drawn vehicles, an easier job as the horse clip-clopped along more slowly.

All these departed things, so thrilling to the Edwardian child, have gone, the magic lantern and the phonograph with its hoarse announcement that this was an Edison Bell record, which was a black cylinder that lived in a green baize lined compartment. The musical box (some were very beautiful) was in most middle class homes, usually under the sideboard. The gramophone ousted the phonograph and the single disc appeared. As an artist I am glad to say that whoever painted the dog listening to a large trumpet (a winner if every there was one, rivalling 'Bubbles' itself) was, I believe, handsomely rewarded. The postcard (½d. stamp) was everywhere. Actresses and well-known people as well as pretty scenes and sentimental pictures were kept in special albums, now quite valuable.

So much has gone, most of it very harmless; those Japanese lanterns at dusk in summer gardens, the coloured glass jars with little candles flickering in the trees and rose arbours. The conservatories, where a little spooning went on, with pink ice cream to cool things off, were bowers of greenery with the scent of roses and tobacco plants wafting in from the garden. Carriages arrived at midnight and coachmen in the big houses stamped up and down or flirted outrageously with pert maids. There was as much 'class' in a maid's apron or a coachman's equipage as there was in Belgravia.

It died, as it had to, as all things die. Except memory...

. . . .

I have been up in the attic of memory and I knew that I should find many old things there. I expected to find a jumble of relics, of souvenirs, of broken objects too precious to throw away. What I did find surprised me and filled me with

"I have painted many butterflies since then..."

Reproduced by courtesy of W.R. Royle Ltd.

wonder and delight. They had not changed. There they were, just as I had left them, all brand new and all so alive, so vital, with the life of my childhood.

I had changed, grown old, but they had not. I stared at them, scarcely believing the reality of what I saw. The clear Edwardian light streamed through the attic window giving a bright purpose to all my childhood connections.

I felt a great uplift of spirit and heard a singing in my heart as once, long ago, I sang with my family all those old familiar songs. The melodies came up from far away with remembered clarity, "Just a song at twilight..." my father was playing while my mother stood by, elegant in deep brown velvet, her hair piled high over the pads she had slipped underneath to give the fashionable Edwardian shape. She wore a cream lace jabot high up her neck, my brothers and I were with her around the piano and we were all singing "...when the lights are low..." I listened entranced, song after song, Victorian and Edwardian, and there was the music in a neat pile in the Memory Attic. I touched the dappled grey rocking horse I once rode so fearlessly, he nodded his head and bowed gently forward.

In the corner stood my mother's dressmaker's dummy, wasp waisted, the bust round and smooth. I saw the little dressmaker who used to call, saw her kneeling down with a packet of shining pins (one farthing's worth) in black folded paper, pinning up the hem of a skirt. "I shall allow for the train, Madam, and allow for the flounce," feminine talk, very mysterious. The flounce was very important; Marie would unpick it when mother came in from the street and wash it. All ladies had flounces on their skirts, outside and inside, under the train to protect the material.

There was our phonograph with the black wax cylinders, each in a neat square hole, quite real, enchanting magic of long ago. Magic? Ah, yes, our magic lantern that father used to entertain us with before the cinema came to Hampstead. There it was with the boxes of coloured slides, 'Jack and the Beanstalk,' 'Little Red

Riding-hood,' 'Babes in the Wood.' My father's voice described the scene and we would sit in the darkness watching the coloured pictures appear, pause while they were described, then glide away — like life itself, full of colour with its vividness and poignancy, so real, so full of meaning, so alive.

It all happened; it is all recorded in my memory. As I stood, alone in the attic, surrounded by all that was once my world, a child's world, I saw that nothing dies unless we wish it to. Now I understand the great Teacher's words — breathless, deathless, changeless — the Spirit abideth forever. I remember as a child taking a little tin bucket to fill with sea water and my surprise at finding that it had no colour. It is we who give things colour and life, we who allow dust to settle upon our hearts. What happens to us? Must time and healing salve repair our own neglect, our foolish discarding of our possessions relegating them to attics as no longer of immediate use but not quite useless?

Now that I am old, divorced from that 'Time', I can look back with tender gratitude to those who gave me birth and their love. I see at last that love is the only reality of life; like the boundless sea, it reflects the colour of the Spirit and it exists, like Memory.

It is what we take with us when we no longer have need of possessions. It is the desireless state, the Kingdom of Heaven that can lie within all mankind. I found it — in the attic.

'Magic World'.

Chapter Five
MARIE~UPSTAIRS, DOWNSTAIRS

" "I know my place and I expect others to know theirs." It is Marie speaking and, although she did not know it, she spoke for the majority of the Edwardians who were emerging into their 'wind of change', a gentle breeze hardly enough to ruffle the long skirts of the women or their ornate hats — or the long white streamers of the house/parlour maids who once graced a scene I knew so well.

Marie was our maid, not our servant, and in countless homes in Edwardian England there were the Maries, part of the family much valued and cared for, and who had immense authority in the home.

She knew her place. Everybody did except for the few who could find no place that fitted them. My place was that of a child, an Edwardian child, and an Edwardian child was to be seen and not heard, to accept what it was told without question, to eat what was set before it and to be obedient. That was a child's place in an era where it seemed everything had a place and there was a place for everything. AND there was Law and Order.

That was Edwardian England and I knew it and grew up in it and as I lift the curtain to remember the scenes of long ago, I also hear Marie say, "I speak as I find". So I will write as I found in a middle class family, where the head of the family was an indulgent and handsome father, clever, wax-moustached, romantic in appearance and utterly beloved by me. My mother was completely in love with him as he was with her all and every day of their lives.

So I had what the Edwardians had in such abundance — security and love.

. . . .

I first encountered Marie when I was aged five. My mother had to undergo a serious operation, serious in those days, and I well remember my worried father saying one morning, "Run up and fetch a cab, my boy." Off I ran, a short distance for the cab rank was close to the railway that was so exciting for a small boy.

"You are wanted at the picture shop," I panted, at the same time saying, "Can I ride up with you instead of inside?"

The inside of a 'four-wheeler' smelt of leather but high up, sitting beside the driver, I found thrilling even if it was only for a few yards. The driver had a long white beard and wore a battered top hat. I had often been sent to fetch cabs for my father's customers and I was fortunate to find him first on the rank. As we clip-clopped to a halt, my mother appeared at the side door. She had a scarf over her head and wore a long quilted dressing-gown reaching to the ground; she was supported by my father at the one side and on the other by our doctor, a very handsome, clean-shaven man. It was he who brought my brothers and me into the world. Immaculate in a glossy top hat, winged collar, cravat, black frock-coat, striped trousers and spats, he held my mother's arm while an anxious young maid followed behind.

I felt I was in a dream for no word of my mother's illness had reached me. Why should children be told anyway? In spite of loving parents, children were to be seen, never heard, and to ask no questions. So mother, pale and weak, was helped across the wide pavement in tiny faltering steps and into the cab together with father and the doctor. The old Hampstead General Hospital was only a hundred yards up the hill; now the Royal Free Hospital stands on the site where, sixty years later, I too became a patient.

My youngest brother and I were sent to our grandparents for three months (I remember we had Christmas there). At the end of that time we were brought home and the next morning I was allowed to see my mother. The ward was large and the nurses seemed tall and starched in white caps, stiff collars and cuffs and they were in dark blue uniforms, skirts reaching to an inch off the floor.

The smell of chloroform pervaded the ward and I was thrilled at last to be taken to my mother. I was hopelessly shy and buried my head in the high bedclothes as she gently stroked my hand. (How strange it is to be writing this when they are all gone — hospital, nurses, doctors, father, mother and two of my brothers.) I recall a lady in the bed opposite beckoning to me. I was much too shy to go over so a nurse carried me across and I was given a piece of butterscotch in shiny silver paper. Why is it that children always remember sweets or food, etc.? A dark-haired girl with her arm in a sling came in with a tray of food. It was Marie and she became my mother's maid having, then, as much influence on me as my teachers at the Kindergarten School.

Marie was Cornish, inclined to moods which she worked off by prodigious feats of washing, scrubbing, sewing or ironing, well up to midnight. She was a tower of strength to my mother and father and I relied on her more and more as my mother got well and father took her off to dances and dinners. Marie's bedroom was next to mine and as I was afraid of the dark she always looked in from time to time. Her very presence and the nightlight sending the shadows flickering softly over the ceiling and bedroom walls were immensely reassuring. Often when she passed to her own bedroom and I could not sleep, she would take me into her own bed and I clung to her nightgowned figure feeling so safe and secure.

I always woke in my own bed in the morning but I loved Marie who seemed so much part of our family. She left years later to get married for she wanted a baby of her own so much that she became almost demented. I said she had a very deep and lasting influence on me and it was to her that I 'escaped' from the grown-ups, the stiff aunts and uncles, into her kitchen. It was always 'her' kitchen and other maids dropped in for a gossip, their charming black and white aproned figures, collars, cuffs and lace caps enchanting me so much that, years later, I painted some pictures to see if I could recapture the memory of Marie and the other maids. When I helped my father deliver some framing orders after eight o'clock at night (it would have been useless to go before as father's clients would have been at dinner) I came in contact with some wonderfully dressed maids. I thought they looked like goddesses, the blackness of their uniforms and the glistening white aprons adorned by the streamers hanging from their beautiful caps. How remote they seemed as they opened the door, the gaslit hall illuminating them. I always begged my father to let me help him for the streets of Hampstead were safe then, safe for a small boy of ten to go out into the deserted streets to deliver parcels. I was so excited when I received the money for the delivered framing orders, usually running all the way back to give father the

". . . other maids dropped in for a gossip . . ."

47

envelope containing the few shillings charged for the work.

I used to recount my adventures to Marie in her kitchen where sometimes I saw a huge policeman (and they were huge) eating a supper that Marie had provided for him. His helmet lay on a smaller kitchen table where Marie put her piles of neat ironing, mostly mother's underwear; Edwardian underwear was very elaborate, lace edged frilly pink ribbon inserted in the petticoats and, unmentionable in those days, the drawers.

To see a policeman's helmet side by side with such an utterly feminine world was a sight I have never forgotten — nor when I was allowed to try it on. It seemed gigantic and very heavy indeed.

Everything in Marie's kitchen was a secret. I never said a word, being too thrilled to share even for a few minutes her warm personality, her loving kindness and her loyalty to our family. I am glad she had her baby daughter, she was so proud; warned not to have another, she would not listen and she died.

"Edwardian underwear was very elaborate..."

Always in my childhood memory, though, Marie was there, there when I returned from school or from painting the autumn leaves, the colours of which fascinated me so much. I would run into the house and clatter downstairs to the kitchen with the child's eternal question, "Where's mother?" "Gone for a soldier," was Marie's reply. I believed it and burst into tears, then she would tell me she was only joking.

My love for her has remained and for all she represented, remained all these years heightened by the passage of time and my understanding of her as a woman as well as just Marie.

When we went on holiday, Marie, of course, came with us. She took me into the bathing machine and undressed me, putting me into a horizontally striped bathing costume. This done she undressed behind a little curtained-off compartment, hanging her own clothes up on a few large iron hooks, her white stays dangling from the laces beside her petticoats, two or three, as well as a long skirt and hat. She emerged in a wondrous bathing costume of deep purple serge with a large collar and sleeves down to the elbows; the skirt fell gracefully over the hips, the lower part coming half-way down the legs and ending with a frill. In the meantime a blue jerseyed man had hooked the bathing machine with chains to a powerful horse and we wended our way down until we were in about three feet of water. Outside were screams of delight from the girls and ladies — it was the women's section, no men were allowed. Their section was at least a hundred yards further down the beach. When the bathing machine stopped and we were ready, we heard the man on the horse retreating to pull down another machine while Marie opened the door facing the sea. What a sight! Dozens of girls and ladies all in the most wonderful bathing dresses (they literally were dresses) with huge rubber caps to cover their hair and all pretending to be frightened as the waves rolled in, translucently pale green mixed with the sand stirred up by many female feet. Some even wore shoes and many had corsets on under the bathing dresses. I never remember seeing anyone swim.

As women and girls can stand cold water far more than men, I was soon shivering and Marie would take me in, dry my thin body and, when she had completed her own dressing which took some time, signal to the man, who came down, hooked up the horses and back we went to the row of empty machines. I loved the sea and any form of swimming and wished I could stand the chill of English sea bathing.

My father would give Marie some money and off we went to buy hot drinks up on the Parade. Mother always took half a house for our holidays; that was a very usual custom and the landlady gave us our meals. They were splendid holidays; minstrels playing banjos and Punch and Judy shows, to say nothing of the pier with the keen fishermen and the slot machines even if I was never allowed to see 'What the Butler saw!' I don't know to this day what it was.

Sometimes when I smell the peculiar aroma of wet sand on wood, I see once again those glorious bathing days with Marie. There is a photograph of my mother and our family taken with another family who were great friends. It shows my mother in her Edwardian summer seaside costume wearing a huge hat piled up with roses, with me, crying for some reason, at her side. A frozen moment in time recalling a vanished past. At home Marie would sometimes take me to

"She emerged in a wondrous bathing costume. . ."

relatives of hers and we would have winkles for tea with a black pin to winkle them out. A great delicacy they were and with the long cos lettuce and some shrimps, the tea was a tremendous success.

. . . .

I think and think, over and over again, of the mystery of my own birth. I try to pierce the wall, try to draw back the curtain that has cut my questioning spirit off from the reality I feel so intensely now I have dug into a privacy that properly belongs only to my father and mother. The Past is so real — the Present is only a dream. I belong to my youth, I am alive only in King Edward's reign; I feel, oh how intensely I feel, with such life, such reality, what I WAS. Even after my third birthday, I became concentrated, solidified into my hated body, a boy's body; as that developed I tried every trick I knew to postpone my life. I hid in Marie, in Marie and her life, for somehow she personified security. In her humble maid's estate I could be whatever I really was; she neither expected me to be a boy or a girl, a failure or a success.

Marie as a maid was part of the family yet not of it. She was cut off by her clothes. My mother and my aunt wore good clothes, huge hats and leg-of-mutton sleeves, and boned bodices tightly hooked over severely corseted figures. In their long bell-shaped corded skirts, their châtelaines jingling, their hair pads to support the luxuriant hair piled over them, they were worlds apart from the world of Marie.

Marie had cheap stays; she told me so. I saw her ironing mother's white and pink stays, saw her iron the long laces and, placing the two well-boned sides apart on her aproned lap, begin expertly to thread the laces. So many times I watched, fascinated. While Marie was ironing, all the other irons were heating up on the round iron top underneath which glowed the kitchen range fire.

Why, oh why, do these scenes crowd into my memory? They are real. I saw them. I can only live when I recall them. It is as if I died when I was breeched, died and was buried. Farewell romance of a little boy, you are too big to cry for Marie now. Too big? You who are so small, so tiny, so shy and so full of nervous fear. Fear of what? Life is what you feared; however dimly, you knew what awaited you. In the shadows of the bedroom fire when you had measles or chicken-pox, in the shadows of the nightlight set in a saucer of water, shadows that danced on the bedroom wallpaper.

High up on the landing outside, the batswing gas jet hissed. . . the hiss and gurgle from the long cupboard in Marie's bedroom. It came from a large square cistern that I thrillingly discovered when I stole into her bedroom.

I was fascinated by her bedroom, her clothes, her dresses hung on the back of the door. The white petticoats hung over the back of the wooden chair, her corsets were rolled up on the chair, her long lace-up boots under the washstand stood up alongside the other pairs of ordinary working shoes. The washstand had a marble

The maid's bedroom.

top with large washbowls and jugs to match standing on it, also the soap dish with its cover to match.

Opposite was her window and under the window a cheap dressing table with little china dishes of hairpins and black ordinary pins. A pincushion like a hedgehog and a china vase to hold the long multicoloured hat pins, her best aprons back from the laundry, crisp, white and glazed with starch — brooding over all this a smell, a warm human smell that strangely reassured me. My heart beat excitedly in Marie's bedroom. I was so young, so frail, so afraid and she was so strong.

I saw her undo her uniform of pink, her working apron lying drunkenly over the chair. Her grey corsets held her body like armour, her tapes, as she called them, of her petticoats firmly tied by her strong hands. She was so dark, a swarthy olive skin showing the Spanish blood in her Cornish body; her lank, dark straight hair hung down her back hiding the top of her stays. She splashed water into the bowl and bathed her face, her armpits framed in lace by her shift. Marie — strong, reassuring Marie.

"Come on," she said, "we're going to my folks for Sunday tea."

I would skip along, excited. We took the tram to Queen's Crescent, only a short ride and a walk through the market. It was a street traders' market with fascinating stalls on barrows, fruit, china, all sorts of things, with straw lying all round about the narrow wooden boxes. Not on Sunday, though, the toiling Edwardian poor rested on the Sabbath day. Men stayed in bed or had a shave in the barbers' shops which were open for some men did not shave at all during the week, just waited for Sunday. In flat caps and chokers they sat reading the Sunday newspapers in wooden chairs, leisurely awaiting their turn.

They had their own shaving mugs on a shelf high up, some even had their own shaving brushes as well. I used to see them through the wide open door on a sunny Sunday; I had immense curiosity. I loved shops and to listen to women picking over secondhand clothes on the market stalls, clothes, cheap toilet things, gaudy pink and blue vases with flowers painted on them, mostly made specially for the markets and all in their cardboard boxes. Some stalls had hats, men's flat caps and black straws for the women. "Ow much this straw, dear?" "Two bob ducks and it's real straw. 'Ere, try it on." And she does; a tired, faded woman, young but so old in the experience of life with her pale, gaunt cheeks and dark ringed eyes. Later in my own life, I heard how many of them felt their husbands' leather belts on a Saturday night. They took to the gin themselves and pawned whatever was pawnable on Mondays to be retrieved the next Saturday. Poverty stalked hand in hand with laughter.

. . . .

The family was the mainspring of the clock that ticked away the Edwardian years. Most homes had at least one maid-servant who held a position in the family life of the middle class that has largely been misunderstood. They came from poor homes and from large families and far from being thought a 'come down' to go into service, these girls valued a good place, as it was called, and became trusted members of the family, often playing an important part in the family life and with a great deal of authority amply backed by the Edwardian mother or father. They bridged a gulf that existed then by reason of the way of life in which children were to be seen and not heard and when discipline was in the very air the child breathed. A code was established and adhered to; it began with the father who was respected and his authority was absolute. It was the mother who softened firm judgements and, since the parents often went out to dine with friends, play solo whist or gossip, it was the maid who took her place and decided how long we might sit up or go to bed. She was in charge and trusted and rarely if ever broke that trust.

In my family the maid left only to get married, returning later proudly to show the mistress the new baby. Downstairs the new maid had put the kettle on, that huge black kettle on the kitchen range, poking up the fire glowing in the middle of the ovens and opening the square tea caddy, that fragrant resource of the British. The tea soon loosened female tongues and the carefully held baby was much admired as it lay in the young mother's arms, spotless in its elaborate gowns of lace and cambric or calico that drooped in Edwardian elegance.

Upstairs tea was formal, best china cups especially if a guest or, more often, an aunt or cousin was present. There was much feminine talk, the guests in clothes so elaborate, their hats a creation of ribbons and artificial flowers, huge hats and several hatpins of great length with ornately patterned heads were carefully pushed through pads over which the long hair was elaborately dressed. A veil which was gently rolled up completed the female head, her gloves were often not removed but unbuttoned and mysteriously pushed back. They all sat bolt upright on formal chairs, their long skirts with the underskirts of taffeta for the desired rustle of petticoats called the 'frou-frou', as they moved with practised grace, their wasp-waisted figures tightly laced into well-boned corsets, 'stays' my mother called them. The bra was unknown but the chemise, an elaborate and necessary garment, was firmly pulled down under the corsets and the lacing up was continued.

The importance of a woman's figure can never be underestimated in any age but in the Edwardian era it dominated a woman's life. It was a symbol of moral uprightness and my mother referred to a woman of easy virtue as 'a loose woman'. For an Edwardian girl not to wear stays, even at a very early age, was as unthinkable as it was for anyone, male or female, to go out into the street without a hat. Even the gypsies who begged at kitchen doors, baby in arms and clothes pegs or white heather in a basket, wore corsets; every street had its corset shop, every newspaper advertised them and the big stores stocked hundreds of pairs of all sizes and colours, all claiming to be so comfortable that a woman would hardly know she was wearing them. Doctors thundered at their pernicious influence without effect — tight lacing was the rage and a girl's ambition was to have a waist span equal to her age. She had a good try to achieve this feminine ambition; by the age of eighteen she hoped to be married and then a little relaxation was but natural!

. . . .

'Upstairs'.

55

As I have said, I was very young when our new maid, Marie, came to work for us; she was immensely strong with a capacity for work bordering on ecstasy. I soon began to associate with Marie's uniform a warmth and a kindly if sometimes rough love, safety and the easy sense of security I craved for.

When she was in her pink print, her sleeves rolled up and her dark hair covered with a white cap, I went carefully. There was work to be done and Marie was a formidable worker, stronger than many a man and in her sulks (for she was inclined to sulk over certain things no one could get her to explain) she would deliberately work well beyond her bedtime. An exaggerated clatter of tins, pots and pans would come floating up and father would say to mother, "Leave her alone and she'll come home wagging her tail behind her". This was a favourite saying of his and very true, for Marie was all smiles the next day and it was "all clear" for me to sneak downstairs and shyly say, ". . . er, Marie?" She would pretend to be grim and tight-lipped and say, "Well. And what do you want?"

". . . Er, Marie, are you in a good mood?"

"Course I am. Ain't I always?"

With an inherited wisdom, I would agree that she was while Marie rested her strong hands on her well-boned hips and looked at me, knowing what I wanted.

"Can I help you?" I would blurt out.

She kept up the game.

"You mean you've been chucked out upstairs, don't you?"

"Not really, Marie. It's just that I like being with you and helping you." This really was true, I did. I felt at home in Marie's kitchen. It was always her kitchen, part of knowing her place and expecting others to know theirs, meaning even my mother or anyone who interfered with what she really regarded as her domain.

Spring cleaning cast a shadow over our lives making my father and brothers as well as myself feel as if we had lost our home. The smell of Lifebuoy soap or Monkey Brand finally died away and the brawny washerwoman, sack aproned, left with her apron rolled up in her basket, half-a-crown safely in her black purse and a bottle of stout under the sack apron, damp from the battle with the copper in the scullery. The steam slowly dispersed out into the garden where huge sheets hung damp from the mangle's wooden rollers alongside nightshirts, huge and usually of striped flannel, shirts, underclothes, chemises but never the unmentionables — the lace edged drawers. These were mysteriously washed and ironed, the pink or blue ribbon was also ironed and threaded on a bodkin to be reinserted in the broderie anglaise that frilled out from the legs as openly flaunted in forbidden music halls by black-stockinged, many-petticoated, laughing 'hussies' as my grandmother called these shocking creatures. There was no strip-tease then but a revealing dance that often ended in a champagne supper in discreet, red-curtained private rooms. Male permissiveness? Certainly. A boy was brought up to 'know' all about life, to hold his liquor like a man and to attain the key of the door on his twenty-first birthday. The young girl? She knew nothing. Her husband would tell her all she needed to know. Even to go to the 'loo' was a carefully contrived affair; one was never to be seen leaving the lavatory, it was both vulgar and unfortunate.

This was the way of life I was trained to behave in and I and my companions would never have questioned the authority that imposed this firm regime. Marie's

"...the intimidating clothes..."

maxim of 'knowing her place' was only an expression of what most people then thought — everyone knew their place. Marie was proud of hers, a housemaid in a family in which she played such an important part, not only in the smooth, efficient running of our home but in my own affectionate regard.

Always I remember her with warm appreciation, her protective figure to which I clung confidingly, trustingly, as I never could to my mother who was kindness itself. A wide gulf existed between children and parents which was never really bridged in spite of, in our case, my father's efforts. The intimidating clothes alone permitted no relaxation; frock coats, high stiff collars, top hats, glossy and shiny, that made my father and uncles look so tall, so far away from a timid little boy who was dressed as a girl.

. . . .

But back to Marie and her kitchen. I loved her so in my childish way. It was true that I hovered around her and to her I went after the dreaded meeting in the drawing room (I used to think it was so named because of the watercolour drawings on the wall, only later learning that it was short for the 'withdrawing' of the ladies when they left the gentlemen to their port and nuts) upstairs which always seemed to be crammed with uncles and aunts, so tall, so correct, so awe inspiring.

I was pulled upon the laps of aunts who were stiff in tight whalebone corsets and high collars often of lace held up by tiny whalebones. These no doubt kindly but formidable ladies would crush me against their whaleboned bodies hung with black jet ornaments that fascinated me and I would hear them remark upon me — the colour of my eyes or hair and whether I took after my father or mother — while black frock-coated uncles boomed out such pleasantries as "And what have you been up to today?" and stared down at me as I shyly said, "How do you do, uncle? I hope you are quite well."

Five minutes of this and my father would say, "Now run along boy."

With what thankfulness I did so, saying good-bye to everybody and quietly closing the door on the murmur of voices in that room with the watercolours on the walls, the mantelpiece with the Sèvres clock and the paired vases on each side, the large mirror reflecting the room with little side trays protruding from its elaborately carved and twisted frame and the many china ornaments.

From this formal atmosphere I gladly escaped to Marie's kitchen which drew me as a magnet — how warm and friendly it was there. Sometimes I would help her to pull and stretch the long lace curtains that every Edwardian home had in every window, six feet long and with a little starch put in the rinsing water, they had to be gently but firmly stretched. I would stand at the end of the kitchen, delighted to be able to assist. Sometimes other maids from nearby houses would pop in and with luck I would not be sent away upstairs to the nursery where the great dappled rocking horse awaited my pleasure.

With the perpetual hunger of childhood, I hovered around Marie as she made cakes and fruit pies, sometimes cadging a small token. A special luxury was to be given the top of a cottage loaf with some of the bread scooped out and the resulting hole filled with condensed milk — it was small wonder I loved dear Marie. Marie seemed to do everything I thought as I haunted her kitchen, her little world. "Don't you dirty my kitchen floor, wipe your feet first..."

I sit in memory watching her, dear Marie, so strong so slight, her neat dark hair under her cap as she irons the Edwardian underwear. In the evening she went round turning down the beds, arranging father's nightgowns and mother's long-sleeved, high-necked nightdress carefully on the bed. Upstairs — Downstairs, everything and everybody knowing their place in that safe, orderly Edwardian world.

Chapter Six
PETTICOATS AND 'APPY 'AMPSTEAD

I was born in a room facing the 'bus terminus. As a very young child it was wonderful for me to watch the tramcars, low single-deck affairs drawn by three horses, one in front of the main pair. It remains an exciting memory to see the passengers embark and the driver change the horses to the front of the tramcar, children begging for the tickets they collected along with cigarette cards. The ladies ascended holding their skirts, with umbrella or parasol in hand, and crossed over to the pavement where father's antique shop was, shaking out their rustling petticoats and proceeding with a stately walk, long skirts trailing and picking up bits of dust and débris in spite of well-swept pavements. Incidentally, it was one of the duties of ladies' maids to unpick the piece of material tacked to the underneath of the skirt hem and sew on a fresh piece so that it was only a strip of material that had to be washed and not a whole dress. I learned this in my talks with Marie, together with a whole lot of domestic information that I found intensely interesting as my interest in costume grew, and useful when drawing and painting the models who wore some of the costumes I collected later.

Sometimes I would hear the clanging of the fire-engines — what a sight! Three horses at full gallop with the large boiler belching smoke at the back, and the crew clinging to the fire engine like Roman gladiators in their huge brass helmets, were followed by the fire-escape ladders on huge wheels. We all ran out to see this magnificent sight, boys pedalling madly behind. There was so little traffic then on quiet Hampstead Heath where now cars stream endlessly to the City and then return, the robot-like figures sitting impassively behind the steering wheels.

In contrast to the dramatic charge of the fire-engine, the milk cart was drawn by a little brown and white Welsh pony. The milk was delivered in pint or half pint metal cans with the lids slammed down over a piece of greaseproof paper; these cans were filled from a large milk churn with a tap unless I carried out a large milk jug which was also filled from the churn with an extra splash for the cat. The horse drew most things except an electric carriage that glided by and the train that came puffing to a halt in a cloud of steam at the nearby station; buses and trams and all delivery vehicles knew only the horse.

Our front window looked out on the horse tram terminus and beyond there was large open space flanked by the railway where exciting locomotives puffed and chuffed as they drew into or away from Hampstead Heath Station. This open space on Bank Holidays was filled with the gypsies and their roundabouts, coconut shies, boxing booths (five shillings offered for any man who could stand up to so-and-so for three rounds) and dark, swarthy gypsy women who told your fortune from your hand — first crossing it with silver. The gypsy women wore huge hats with three coloured ostrich plumes drooping over the wide brims; the dark skinned men had hooked noses and all boasted that they were real Romanies. They came in their carved, painted and gilded caravans and soon up went the swings and roundabouts, gaudy in gold paint and scrolls with lions and tigers handpainted on any square yard of space.

There were coconut shies, three balls a penny — ''Roll up, roll up, half way for ladies'' — hoop-la, shooting ranges, also the double-headed sheep and the

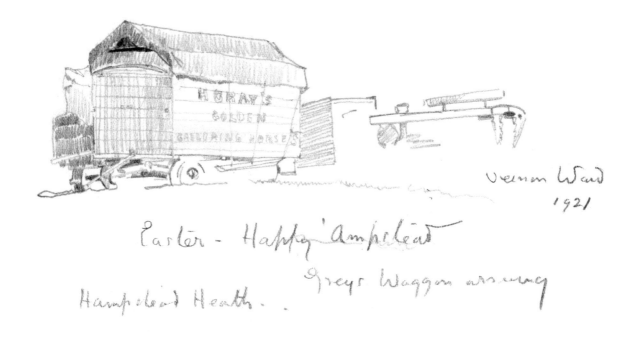

Easter - Happy 'Ampstead
Hampstead Heath.   Greys Waggon arriving

Vernon Ward
1921

armless lady. I marvelled at her as she cut paper patterns with her toes, poured herself a cup of tea and drank it!

Ah, the innocent eye beholding these wonders. First, while very young, I could only watch from our drawing room window. The crowds that came up from all parts of London were so dense, so colourful, sailors in wide trousers, soldiers in scarlet and neat little black pill-box hats, coster girls and factory girls all wearing their best aprons, and 'the Pearlies', a wonderful sight simply smothered in buttons, riding on their little donkey carts. All the fun of the fair ran riot and the noise was simply deafening as steam-driven roundabouts with their gaily carved and gilded horses circled the watching crowd. The girls rode side-saddle of course, showing those provocative petticoats with an eye on the sailors and soldiers or young men who had come to ''date up'' these feminine tender traps and who crowded round waiting. Some, not so feminine (or two for they generally moved in pairs), stood up (forbidden!) in the swing boats and sent the boat higher and higher, petticoats really showing this time, to the admiration and encouraging yells of the crowd.

The 'glory' has departed now and the famous 'Appy 'Ampstead is a mechanical ghost of its former colourful past.

. . . .

Gypsy families, some I believe of considerable wealth, ran the main amusements and I experienced this during the war when prices soared from twopence and threepence a ride on the roundabouts to one shilling and sixpence, a considerable sum in those days. The gypsy women were so dark and so colourfully dressed, in large hats with those real ostrich feathers adorning them, silk blouses, wasp-

Bank Holiday
Hampstead

Vernon Ward
1921

Hampstead Fair.

Vernon Ward 1921

61

waisted figures of which they, as most women, were intensely proud.

One of the amusements was a contrivance consisting of a huge red and yellow plank some twenty or thirty feet in height. This was an irresistible attraction to the men, be they soldiers, sailors or just young civilians. The procedure was invariably the same; for the price of a penny one was handed a huge yellow mallet, and he who came to show his strength spat on his hands and handed his jacket to his girl if he was a 'civvie'. (No soldier or sailor ever removed his jacket, it was forbidden by regulations.) Then, with his eye, he would measure the loose iron knob in a wooden structure about two feet high. Up would go the hammer and down it came with a crash upon the knob; on the plank were markings in feet and a large object would slide upwards. The trick was to hit the knob squarely and with great force. If it went right up, it rang a bell fixed at the top. There were ''oohs'' and ''aahs'' and gasps of female admiration from the little crowd. The coster girls in their huge hats wore the aprons proudly showing their class. The pig bladders on sticks or the 'ticklers' all designed for 'getting off' were everywhere. Men, boys, girls, women, all bought one — an 'Appy 'Ampstead introduction card.

The Fair was jammed with people whose drab lives were spent in the East End shops or the factories in Whitechapel and the Old Kent Road. Up they came by the thousand and by midday the streets were almost impassable. Factory girls, sometimes sixteen abreast, cleared everyone out of their advancing path, singing all the music hall songs at the tops of their voices, and wearing three-quarter length skirts the better to show the high laced boots and for the penny skipping rope display. Display was the word, for jumping over the huge rope gave the girls every chance to show those lace-edged petticoats and neat ankles. As the rope went higher and higher to encouraging cries of ''Go it girl, show 'em,'' lace-edged drawers came into view and an absolute froth of white petticoats that swirled like the sea breaking over the rocks.

The girls queued up to display their talents, hoping to 'get off' with a nice young man to share the Bank Holiday with. They worked terribly hard for so little money but their day was Bank Holiday, the Fair fluttered with prizes, the carved horses were there to ride, all to the blaring music. The factories were silent while the Heath resounded with the laughter of Edwardians on holiday, holidays that were so rare, looked forward to and saved up for. The pubs were jammed but the police were tolerant — nobody wanted to arrest anyone. The swings were filled, the girls standing up to make them swing the higher, once again those petticoats being used as feminine ammunition. Jellied eels on small china plates with slices of lemon and vigorously shaken bottles of vinegar were devoured, likewise the oysters and other delicacies from the food stall which also provided lemonade in huge glass tanks. All the fun of the Fair!

An amusement that disappeared from the 'Ampstead scene was sliding down the wire. A strong wire was stretched from a platform up which girls as well as men climbed to await their turn to slide down. They were handed an iron contraption that had a wheel on it and the man in charge clipped it on the wire. It had two wooden handles protruding from it and, firmly grasping it, one slid down the wire to land, feet outwards, against a padded board — the forerunner of hang-gliding? Of course, the girls found this most exciting as, high above the

Entrance to Well Walk
Hampstead

Vernon Ward 1921

Houses in Well Walk

63

Vernon Ward
1921

Hampstead Village

Vernon Ward. 1921.

Hampstead Village

Old Houses
Hampstead - Vernon Ward - 1921.

From — "My 'selves' when young"

The full moon now. Why does that play such an important part in my life? It has, from my earliest recollections. I crouched by the edge of the Hampstead Pond at night. I had to. I was compelled to. To steal out quietly, never to tell anyone. To crouch down upon my heels and watch in silence the reflection of the moon.

I was ageless then. No more a child. I had no parents, no school, no body... I was me.

I stared and stared at the silver disc. I felt the mystery of being alive and being happy. No, not happy — that word belongs to this earth. I was myself and I was fulfilled.

I belonged — but to whom? I never asked that question. I obeyed a call more powerful than reason could explain, and I kept it my secret. I can safely say that those years of my early childhood squatting at the water edge with the starlit world above me were my only reality. I did not want an explanation. I saw nothing in the moon's reflection and I did not want to see anything. But the world was of a purpose and I was me and that was sufficient. Later it died away, the urge to sit on my heels I mean, but I always stopped and looked up.

There in the sky she was, riding like a Goddess, bright and silvery. Sometimes she broke through dark, racing clouds, my silver moon, so remote, so pure, so much part of my life.

I still look up, I still feel that all is well. My dislike of life upon earth is smoothed away. The deep hurt, the constant loneliness of my real self, the hidden, secret self, is dissolved by the moon and the immensity of dark, starlit eternity above me.

The people fade away, I know of the impermanence of life on earth. It is utterly unreal to me.

Vernon Ward, Hampstead, 1977.

admiring crowd, they glided across with screams of female joy. Did it occur to them that the admiring crowd underneath had a perfect view of those petticoats and the ribbon-inserted drawers?

As night came on the whole scene became a bright and glorious revel, the naptha flares hanging from the booths, the roundabouts, swings and everything possible, lighting up the flushed faces of the factory girls, free.. for one wonderful Bank Holiday Monday, Easter, Whitsun and finally August.

As the night went on fortune tellers were in great demand. Tents masked the interviews, silver crossing the palm and prophesies of dark strangers. Outside, gypsy women had a tray of cards, each with a fortune printed on it, and a budgerigar would pick one out with his beak while everyone laughed. There would be some drunkenness and the police would come with their long carts and strap down some fighting drunk who wouldn't go away. Midnight still found many crowds, in pairs by now. The little street stalls were gone leaving a litter of straw, trampled cardboard and shavings — oh, what a mess to be cleared up in the morning. The heath keepers would pile up the débris and make bonfires of the rubbish while the fish had a party with the bits of bread floating on the ponds.

The lights stayed late in the painted caravans, 'vans' as the real gypsies called them. I used to draw them in pencil, my father dragging me out of bed, sleepy-eyed, at six in the morning. Marie was up and had tea, hot and steamy, ready for us and off we went. I painted these scenes many times. Where are they now?

What subjects! No wonder Dame Laura Knight and Sir Alfred Munnings painted this incredible painter's scene. I had a lot to with these Romany folk later for, when the 1914-18 war broke out and as the yearning to forget those casualty sheets we all scanned each day grew stronger, the Hampstead Fair did a roaring trade charging one shilling and sixpence at the peak hours. By then the blaring steam driven roundabouts, the swing boats, and the conical helter-skelter had queues. There was khaki then instead of red coats and the navy wore sailor collars and horizontally creased wide trousers. The girls had shorter skirts and an air of desperation crept in.

Actresses strutted up and down on the Music Hall stages singing that on Monday they walked out with a soldier, on Tuesday with a tar. Female recruiting sergeants handed white feathers to any man in civvies. Some dreadful mistakes were made and so was a lot of money. The gypsies came into Father's shop and thought nothing of thirty or forty guineas for a Dresden china figure while we were steadily going broke. I used to deliver these beautiful objects to the 'vans'. ''It is the green one, son, you can't miss it'', and I carried the fragile burden, carefully wrapped in scrunched up newspaper, then sheets of virgin white tissue paper and finally brown paper with string tied in a special knot that came untied with a tiny pull.

Beset by snarling curs which snapped ferociously while chained underneath the van, I called out to the half-opened door with its wreath of curling smoke. A hoarse voice yelled at the dogs and bade me come up. Inside was a neat, tidy home, lace curtains, beds folded back, a mantelpiece, a little oven and, by one of the windows swagged with lace, a shelf. On it were vases or tinselly objects that made me blink — such incredible taste I found impossible. Then I unwrapped the Dresden china as they made a space for it by pushing the hideous vases closer together. Their delight in its subtle beauty, in the china lace sleeves of the figure, somewhat mitigated what I knew my father felt; he hated parting with beautiful things but we hardly averaged five shillings a week in the first years of the war. He still saw the picturesque qualities of the caravans, the tether-ponies, many of them piebald, the gaudiness of the shooting galleries with little ping-pong balls rising and falling on jets of water and the hoop-la stalls with more hideous vases and bowls of goldfish or a fair-haired doll — hard to ring with the little hoops that would only just fit over the prize.

It was in the great days of the Hampstead Fair, a veritable green lung for pale faced but sturdy young men and women. At night the bright lights (for electric motors were coming in then) reflected the centre portion of the Fair in the Hampstead ponds. After midnight folk began to drift homewards and the 'fair-men' began to dismantle the roundabouts, booths and swings. In the morning a huge traction engine towed away caravans and vehicles piled high with coloured poles or gilt horses, red nostrilled, scarlet painted seats and bright red leather reins.

The 'petticoats' were gone or walked slowly away, arm in arm, in deep conversation, dark shadowy figures, the night covering all up like a black skirt covering those lace-edged petticoats to come out another time. But as the years went on, there came changes and, in 1914, the biggest change Europe was to know for a long time. Black armbands were worn by everyone — it was to have been 'all over by Christmas'. We had moved to where I sit writing now; it is very quiet. Outside is 'Appy 'Ampstead. Petticoats are few now, non-iron and almost a joke, lace is a bit of a gimmick, a sewn on quarter or perhaps half inch. The policemen seem very young but their burdens are many. But I did see 'Appy 'Ampstead for many years and am glad, so very glad, that I did. What the Edwardians had in abundance, in overflowing abundance, was the gift of laughter as well as peace though many had precious little to laugh about. But there was peace and the winds of change were gentle and slow.

. . . .

Something of the spirit of a 'Appy 'Ampstead was reflected in the life of the Edwardian streets. There was a warm, human feeling about those streets in my childhood days with the little German bands on the street corners, fathers and sons usually in groups of four or five, playing out their stock of musical tunes with a slightly military flavour. The musicians were always in dark green uniforms and very polite as they received the pennies generously given by their audience.

The organ grinder was the most popular; he wound the handle and out came the mechanical clatter of stimulating music while we stood around entranced by the little monkey in his scarlet jacket perched on top of the barrel organ. This endearing little half-human, sweet animal would go round with his tiny cap held out for the penny almost everyone would give, then he would hand the cap to his master to the delight of the small circle. Children, mainly little girls in the inevitable pinafores and hats, would dance together to the music. How grave they were! I can see them now, these small girls, enjoying life as they found it and I will say that, although it was hard and disciplined with poverty everywhere, there was always this naïveté, the peculiar quality I associate with my childhood. There was a humanity and kindliness, not only among the poor or the housemaids that were such a warm part of my life, but in all those with whom I came in contact. Charity was urged upon child and adult, the churches were full every Sunday for the Edwardians still went to Church. The sermons were on charity and morality as they still are today, but there were more of the faithful to listen.

The street cries were another feature. ''Oh, won't you buy my sweet blooming lavender'', was delightful to listen to; I seem to remember fifteen bunches for a penny but perhaps I have that wrong. Knives to grind — ''Knives ter grind, knives ter grind, any old sizzers or knives'' — out would come the housemaids, bearing scissors, carving knives or whatever, all to be sharpened by the good humoured man sitting at his contraption. This was a large stone wheel with a tin of water above it at which he pedalled energetically so that the stone wheel revolved; breathlessly we watched him while the maids exchanged gossip. Life, human life, human contact was everywhere, in the crowds of children enthralled by the Punch and Judy Show or the Salvation Army, that blue uniformed circle of dedicated men and women inspired to help their fellow men in more ways than their prayers and the rousing music that we heard in the street.

There were the costers, the flower sellers, the rag and bone men and the barrow boys. On Sundays we used to hear the bell of the muffin man and the maids in their black and white, white lace caps with streamers and stiff white cuffs, would emerge from the gaslit halls and buy the muffins the man carried on his head in a wooden tray covered with a white cloth. Then there was the lamplighter, a neat trim bowler-hatted sprite of a man who thrust his magic pole into the hole under the gaslight which would spring into a bright green light in the gathering dusk.

Street cries, street trading, street entertaining — how colourful were those Edwardian streets! And they were safe, safe and friendly. The huge policemen were there more to lend a helping hand than to make arrests yet always there was Law and Order hand in hand with love and laughter.

"Who'll buy my lavender?"   *Reproduced by courtesy of Solomon & Whitehead Ltd.*

'Fresh cut flowers'.   Reproduced by courtesy of Solomon & Whitehead Ltd.

'*Primroses — yellow primroses*'.   *Reproduced by courtesy of Solomon & Whitehead Ltd.*

Chapter Seven
SCHOOLDAYS

I become a schoolboy. To write this chapter in my life is one that I dread for previously I have written of the Kindergarten, of Miss Slipper and Miss Helen, and of the maids and nurses who took us to school. I have written of that word that is part of a woman's make-up, the word 'security'. I speak generally, of course, but to a woman security is still part of her, like her awareness of herself. Then came the day when my father took me to school.

The school he would have liked me to go to was a smaller public school where the son of one of his clients went but he also had two other sons to think of and could not afford it. So the day came (I suppose I was by then about eight) when I went with my father to interview the Head of a school at Highgate, just before the great Archway Bridge. The very sight of it, a huge grey block of hideous design so utterly different to all I had known, was the beginning of the worst and most hellish period in all my hardworking, 'conned', and bewildered life. Although my father was of no recognised religion, preferring to think for himself, this was a Roman Catholic college because he was too poor to send me to a better school. I hated and detested every hour of this monstrous existence!

We walked down the few stone steps of the college and rang the bell, that bell for whom it tolls... The door was opened by a small man wearing a cassock, a red cross in cloth on the breast and a rosary tucked into the black leather belt he wore round his waist. We went into a stone cold, bare hall with the man who later I learned to call Brother as all the masters were — Brother James, Brother Alphage, Brother Justice and the rest. We were interviewed by little, sharp-nosed Brother Conleith who was deputising for the Brother Superior.

Looking back I can see that I rather liked Brother Conleith and his Irish accent. Several of the Brothers were Irish, the Irish seemed to take to Roman Catholicism as I took to drawing. Why I shall never know and neither do I care but I was duly enrolled and was to start when the college reopened.

I walked with my elder brother and a friend, two miles over Parliament Hill, up Swains Lane, past Highgate Cemetery where so many famous people lie. The body of Elizabeth Siddall (a 'stunner' as Dante Gabriel Rossetti had described her to Millais) was exhumed on a dark night in order to retrieve his poems, for in his remorse at leaving her alone to die, Rossetti had buried them with her. The little red-haired milliner's assistant is in many of Rossetti's paintings. He even taught her to draw quite well, too.

I continue to put off writing of my hatred for this school where in silence I suffered so, so much that even the name, the sight of a monk or priest or nun makes all sense of fairness leave me.

God, how I hated Christianity! How I loathed the prayers, the sign of the Cross, the long rows of desks, the smell of ink, the blackboard and those cassocked teachers, some with little black skull caps and all with that bald, shaven patch on the top of the head. The very sound of the clinking rosary, the ghastly crucifixes with the horrible figure nailed on the cross, the hours of scripture, the image of God as an angry, grey-beared patriarch who had invented or created Adam, made the Tree of Knowledge, then, like a sadistic Sergeant-Major, made it 'out of bounds' — hatred swirls over me as I recall the horrible memories.

Scripture, scripture, scripture! Prayer to begin the day, the Sign of the Cross, Hail Mary full of grace... a world I could never believe in. Even as a small boy I felt it all utterly unreal and I still do though I appreciate the Bible with its solemn beauty and its strange listing of wars, an angry God and Prophets crying, ''Woe, woe.'' Where are they all now? Aesthetic Brother Conleith, Brother Alphage, Brother Justice, Brother James who made my life a Hell for the year I was in his class and Brother Superior, old Tut-tu-tues? (''Touch your toes''.) Sometimes we were sent to him, a kindly grey-haired stout and elderly man, the Head in his book-lined study. We bent over, touched our toes and got six stinging cuts on the behind; smarting but gritting teeth, for to cry was to commit a crime, we went slowly back to our classrooms, later to show our weals to awestruck boys in the lavatories. ''Does it hurt?'' ''No.'' As if one would admit that it hurt like hell.

Nobody minded, it was always a just punishment and he was kind afterwards. It was the yelling savages of all ages kicking footballs about, that clanging bell summonising us to that horrible classroom, the rows of desks, the long blackboard, the scratch of white chalk and the incomprehensible figures and writing — I never understood any of it any more than I understood God.

Every day was a small hell. Two miles to walk there, two miles back after the four o'clock bell had rung, satchel laden with two hours homework for I was a day boy while most were boarders. My school life was a dread, a succession of fears — I thought it would never end. I died every time I opened my desk and put my jam or banana sandwiches in with the Latin primer, the English grammar and my exercise books. I felt and was an alien, a Protestant in a Catholic school.

The Brothers were dedicated teachers. They had nothing except their rosaries, cassocks and snuff which they took out of little boxes and sniffed, first up one nostril and then the other. I watched, fascinated with horror, as I sat at a desk in one of the youngest classes and began to learn Reality. Reality or Fantasy? As I grew used to being in this gigantic school of three hundred boys, I wondered sometimes if it was all a bad dream.

They gave a fine education, these dedicated men, but the Holy Mother of God seemed to be everywhere and the Catechism, which we all had to learn by heart, contained all the answers a Roman Catholic needed to know. It hasn't altered much even today. Roman Catholics fight and murder each other still, just as hundreds of years ago, when Bloody Mary married Philip of Spain and tried to impose upon England the religion of Spain which ended with the Armada. The Inquisition was in full swing in those terrible times after Henry VIII had broken with Rome, confiscated the riches of the church and triggered off burnings, murder and bitter hatred. It has died away now because this country has learned of other religions, of Islam, of Buddhism and more, but in my youth a multiracial attitude was non-existent.

I remember the altar at St. Joseph's, 'Holy Joe's' as the more ribald called this fine, green-domed structure with the lighted candles glittering in the semi-darkness, the colourful ritual, the swinging censer emitting its pungent lovely smell. I sat and listened, comprehending nothing, yet I learned a great deal about the Roman Catholic way of thinking or rather, lack of it, for a good Roman Catholic never thought at all. He or she accepted what they were told with no arguments. ''Thou art Peter and upon this rock I will build my Church'', Jesus was supposed to have said and that was that. Not for me, though, I dared to think for myself and still do. I believe in a Creator but, like William Blake, I wonder that He who made the Tiger also made the Lamb. But when I went to my school, every day with friends we met at the top of Parliament Hill, we were just heedless schoolboys; I never spoke much about the difference in our religion but silently I watched, silently I observed and on Sunday afternoons I used to leave our house and go and listen to the celebrated Father McNab who preached on Parliament Hill.

Father McNab was a very well-known preacher, almost a Cardinal, and I used to stand outside the little knot of dumb people listening to him. Once when he invited questions, shy as I was, I spoke up from the little ring of listeners and he courteously replied. I argued with him, tried to trap him, but always he outwitted me. His was a thin, aesthetic figure, his worn eager face with his burning fanatical eyes caught my interest. Only a few years ago, I saw a full length portrait of him; there he was, standing as I had known him, telling us of the grace of God that was available to all who loved Him. He ended the talks with a prayer and the sign of the cross that was so familiar to me.

He was a good man and a very learned, clever man. I wish now I had been older and talked to him; some part of me always stood apart from life and he would have understood this better than the cloistered Brothers no one could become close to, certainly not in that living hell of a school.

Always I have seemed to be two people. One part tried, even to enduring that college for him, to be what my father wanted me to be; the other and much more important part was the one who loved Marie, lived in her world, shared her life, cuddled up to her warm body when as a frightened little boy she took me into her bed, sat watching her ironing and watched her sewing, fingers holding the fabric and needle flying in and out. Marie. Marie's world downstairs. Marie taking me in a bathing machine at the seaside, giving me Nestlés milk in the top of a cottage loaf. That part of me is ageless, the school part is dead even though it may come back to haunt me...

Editors' note: It is interesting and significant that nowhere has Vernon left any drawings or paintings that could in any way relate to those hated school days. There are countless nostalgic Victorian and Edwardian paintings and sketchings, memories of childhood, of the maids, the kindergarten, of everything relating to his earlier life and, later, of the war and his life with Noël Syers and other contemporaries. School was just too unpaintable...

Chapter Eight
'SALAD DAYS' AT THE SLADE

I was taken to the Slade School of Art, University of London, in 1919 at the tender age of fourteen and a half. I believe, up to then, the famous portrait painter, Ambrose McEvoy, who was fifteen when he was accepted, was the youngest pupil to have this privilege.

My father was not a little proud of his son's talents which had, from the age of five or six, had so much encouragement, not only from George Fox but from the well-known Helen Allingham, Knowles the figure painter, Childe Pocock who taught at the Central School of Art, plus many other artists who patronised my father's corner of shops and who were always ready to help and advise me. There were, too, a few sad cases of artists who had failed but who had great talent who came to my wonderful father for a few shillings to keep them going. They, too, gave me singularly fine practical advice as well as artistic help.

In those days people still walked to their work for walking was a Victorian custom as any reader of Dickens will know. He thought nothing of twenty miles just for exercise with his guests at Gads Hill. I was going to that wretched school at Highgate, walking two miles there and back, and George Fox, when he came to paint the Dickensian subjects I have mentioned, often walked from his lodgings at Croydon. We thought nothing of walking and we saw far more deeply by reason of not travelling by motor car.

My precocious involvement with drawing and painting and the many pictures my father made me copy fostered still further this capacity for really seeing. I have one copy that staggers me when I think I was only fourteen when it was painted and another of a Harlequin that made my father exclaim, ''That settles it. You have the three qualities necessary for an artist.'' (His opinion, not mine.) He went on, ''First the imagination without which you will be just a hack. Second a sense of colour that is true and correct and, third, the desire, utter devotion or compulsion to become an artist.''

We gathered together some charcoal drawings executed in the 'stippled' method, a few landscapes which I passionately loved to paint and one or two figure studies for which my father had posed in costume on Sundays. This we used as our selection to show to the Principals of the Slade.

Needless to say, it was a very shy, nervous small child who, with his father, came trembling into the quadrangle of London University where, on the left side, was the famous Slade. It was the spring of 1919. We waited in a corridor with four or five other new entrants ('freshmen', I believe, is the correct term) outside the Principal's door. In a few moments that seemed like an hour, we were told to go in.

Sitting in that rather awesome room were the masters ready to interview me. All were without beards. Standing, tall and thin with a stern face, was Professor Henry Tonks with the white streak in his otherwise dark hair that almost seemed another part of his unique personality. Sitting was a sturdy, jovial sort of man who was Wilson Steer, the man Tonks admired above all others. Another smallish, slightly saturnine man was the famous portrait painter, Sir Walter Russell, and by his side, a kind faced, youngish man with an artificial leg, possibly the result

Probably two of Vernon's earliest flower paintings, dated 1919, the year he went to the Slade.

of a war wound. I pay everlasting tribute to this kind, charming drawing master who taught me and who was so patient with me in my three months' drawing in the 'Antique'. This was what we called the large room where men and women worked side by side though, of course, they never mixed. In the life class and in the quarter hour breaks, it was always 'ladies first'.

My turn came to be examined. One by one father produced my boyish efforts, handing them to Professor Tonks who held them up for all the examining masters to see. (I omitted to mention another very kind man called Charlton who, at over ninety, is still with us.)

It was just after the Great War. The man who seemed so huge in Somerset Maughan's *Of Human Bondage* where he describes two American art students walking about in beards and corduroy trousers would perhaps understand how a little schoolboy of fourteen and a half felt when the masters nodded their approval as each childish effort was handed round. For the first time in my life I saw my beloved father vanquished.

Professor Tonks, looking rather like Sherlock Holmes, suddenly said to my father, "All right, we accept him. Let him start to-morrow!"

My father, who was one of the most sarcastic men I had up to then encountered when he felt that way, gulped and said to Tonks, "But my son is going abroad to finish his education and learn French. He is only a child."

Tonks turned on his heel and from his great height said in a sour voice, "An artist doesn't need any education. He educates himself."

This I have found to be completely true. And so (Good-bye Highgate) I was enrolled at the famous art school, the best in England, and in this provocative statement I include the Royal Academy Schools where the assertion will no doubt be hotly disputed.

Sir William Orpen and Augustus John have been star pupils, their marvellous life drawings hanging framed on the walls, and in my time we had Monnington, Guthrie, Robin Burns and others of equal fame. Francis Marshall became a friend of mine and Stanley Spencer, who was having a refresher course, was particularly kind to me. There were many others who have made their mark in the art world; Rex Whistler was given full scope for his genius and the Tate Gallery's refreshment room décor bears witness to this enormously talented man and to the folly of the Army in letting him lose his valuable life on the beaches of Normandy.

So I commenced to work in real earnest. I haunted the Victoria and Albert Museum with Francis Marshall, the celebrated fashion draughtsman of *Vogue* who also produced those lovely drawings of famous Society people in the Michael Arlem period. His 'Green Hat', a sensational bestseller, gives a very accurate assessment of the modes and manners of the twenties.

The women students of the Slade, the avant-garde, were all dressed in huge black hats and black flowing cloaks trying to look like Augustus John's long-skirted models. I worked very hard in the 'Antique', first on the skeleton hanging up. At one time, I knew every bone — the cranium, jaws, neck, vertebrae, the ribs, the sternum, the clavicles, the head of the humerus and the humerus itself, the radius and ulna and the wrist bones, the pelvis, the femur, the portella, the tibia and fibula, feet, ankles, the lot. There were the outside muscles, too — deltoid, sterno-mastoid, sternum, thorax, pelvis. I only state this because it was part of the training before we entered the 'Antique' to draw the Venus de Milo, the Discobles and many figures, male and female, all copies in white plaster. The training was extremely thorough and there were no short cuts; either we could draw or we could not. As Professor Tonks would have said, "Why come here and waste our time if you do not intend to WORK?"

The young Vernon Ward at his easel.

The young student.

About once a week we used to go into the anatomical theatre where specimens of dead bodies came up for inspection and instruction from the University College Hospital opposite. This structure (that is, the theatre) was a sort of round pit. The lecturer and assistant stood by a wooden table below and we sat, men and women students (mainly, of course, medical), and we were instructed literally in the bare bones of the figure! The specimen's arms and legs and very private parts were handed to us covered with butter muslin on a white dish which we passed on to each other. I remember a girl I worked side by side with and liked so much, turning scarlet as I handed to her, with a perfectly straight, proper face, the private parts of a man who had just recently died. Even in the 1920s most of the girls were extremely modest; it was Mark Twain who said that man is the only animal that can blush — or has need to!

When, after three months, I was adjudged good enough to go down to the life class for two afternoons a week, I had my first sight of a naked woman. I walked in, drawing board under my arm; I suppose I was fifteen years old by then. The whole of the men's class was working hard, those nearest the wooden platform on which the model sat had themselves to sit on what is technically known as an artist's 'donkey' which is an elongated wooden stool with a support for the drawing board. One sat astride it and drew the model but for some of the women students wearing the now fashionable short skirts, this was rather uncomfortable and impractical.

As she was the first nude woman I had seen, and there is a vast difference seeing a painted nude on canvas or a statue to a real live woman with operation scars and all, I blushed so much that I hardly knew how to draw her. Mr. Charlton came up and put me at my ease, explaining in quite matter-of-fact tones how to construct the figure remembering the 'big forms' and the shading and telling me to bring out the form and not get lost in detail. He showed me the careful method and I copied his style. The next afternoon Gilbert White came in and his method was a little different. Next time in came Mr. Wheatley who later became Professor at the Slade and who taught me to ignore all I had been told and to draw the space between the arms and legs and so on. Walter Russell sat down, looked at my careful drawing, drew marks all over it, boomed ''Construct!'' and walked away.

Finally, by which time I was trembling with fear and bewilderment, came the dreaded Tonks. How I wish I still had the drawings of this superb master that he drew beside my pitiable efforts. I had lots of them, three years of hard work, which I kept in a cupboard for many years. When I went to the cupboard they, together with some threatrical costumes, were just a sodden mass — the cupboard had dry rot. The whole lot were thrown away in a dreadful condition, a great mistake as I know now that some could have been dried out and saved.

At that time I was to be a second John Constable as landscape came as naturally to me as Freud and Jung to the psychiatrists or psychologists. How times change. Of course young men and women, and there is still a difference, go to art schools just as I did and, no doubt, still scrape the paint off their palettes and wipe it on the wall. Beware of leaning against those walls. I have never returned to the Slade for which I am sorry, for I was far too shy and the after-effects of the War were in full blast as it were.

I often wonder, when I hear of the interest shown in perfectly blank canvases on exhibition at extortionate prices or the one coloured blue all over, whether it is not time for me to hang up my palette, draw social security along with my old-age pension and sit and dream, dream of my youth, of all those dead friends and helpers of a shy little boy in a cheap brown suit (£4 from Kentish Town) and a brown trilby hat.

Not content to do our stint at the Slade, my friend Marshall and I used to go off and draw at the Victoria and Albert Museum where I had a reader's ticket. We used to study and make notes from the wonderful collection of books there; it seemed that we just could not study hard enough. I was too young to become involved in the 'rags' the Slade students got up to against King's College. I know one day I was aghast as I saw what the students, no doubt King's, had done in the night to the London University. The outside railings were alternately pink and blue and at the foot of the grand stone staircase were two bronze statues on whose heads were stuck the paint pots. It was just high spirits. One girl who went along actually had her arm broken. Because I was such a child, I was not allowed to go; I made up for it when I went to the now defunct Chelsea Arts Ball but that is another story.

I cannot help thinking when I hear, see or read of all that goes on today, the sawn-off shotguns, the actual claiming of responsibility for murders and the perils of Hampstead Heath at night, that once I walked there at any hour in perfect safety, sometimes waiting all night to see the dawn come up from the top of Parliament Hill. How safe Hampstead was then — a few couples under the bushes, a tramp or two fast asleep — the sun piercing the mist and fogs over the City of London. Even after the end of that stupid war run by stupid people and fought by the bravest of the brave of all nations, there was still a sanity in the art I was trained for, to draw the human figure so that it was a human figure, to paint a sky that looked like a sky, a river that reflected the trees, rushes and passing barges, a horse that actually had four legs, a head and a nose, or the portraits of dogs I drew gladly for five shillings a time.

There was a real hunger then as I suppose there is today, but often I wonder if the BBC dare get out the recording of John Hilton who spoke once a week on the distresses of the miners and cried and cried as he read out the letters he received. I, too, began to know the utter falsity of governmental promises; it is all part of Art. Art began when the first cave dweller smeared his finger in coloured clay and made the first doodle, far back in time before the great God we call Computer, before the machine to make the machine, and when artists and craftsmen gained real satisfaction from doing beautiful work. I urge the restless, television drugged, brainwashed populace to go to the art galleries and see real painting or the craftsmanship of a beautiful snuff box or pomander that kept out the smell of the London that was.

It is a curious thing that we who pride ourselves on our advancement, yet still don't know how the pyramids are built or whence came the ring of stones at Avebury, produce such things as Centrepoint in Tottenham Court Road or the dreadful, horrible architecture that poor humans are supposed to live in today. The artist has his place in social life; he does not have to be a drugged drop-out as in so many plays offered to a bewildered, decent public as entertainment.

There is such a thing as job satisfaction; there is such a thing as creating something beautiful for pleasure and not for money. Was it not Albrecht Dürer who, sadly, died at such an early age who said, "I know not what Beauty is, but this I do know. If the student will devote his whole soul and mind to Nature, Nature in return will reward him with an entirely new vision."

It is true, I have proved it over my long life. I am amused to see the value now put on antique things. Why? Because they were made by craftsmen who had served a hard seven years' apprenticeship before doing anything. It has all been taken over by machines now, technology is the word invented. It had to come and the result is anger, jealousy, spite, fear of war and the lies of politicians; the country has lost its way. May it find it, is my prayer at the end of this chapter, and may God help this god forsaken land.

Chapter Nine
AFTER THE SLADE

When the time came for me to leave the Slade School of Art, I was very much like the seven-year apprentice.

I could undoubtedly draw the human form and construct it, which is absolutely essential. I knew all the bones of the skeleton and their functions and I was familiar with the top surface muscles that cover the human body. I also learnt that the male had not the same amount of fat, surface fat, as the female had and that the female pelvis was wider, presumably for child-bearing purposes, also that the necks of the femur bones projected more from the side of the pelvis thus enabling the female to sit on the ground, legs stretched out, with the sort of physical ease that the male is unable to achieve. If one studies people relaxing on the ground, a picnic is a good example, the observer will see that the female sits upright far more comfortably than the male. In 'modern' so-called art, this knowledge is probably superfluous like drawing and all the essentials taught to the art student of the 'twenties.

Without getting into a dispute with the art critics (the teachers?), the hangers on who cluster round the world of art and earn the contempt of the practising professional artist, I feel I can say that, without a real purposeful training, all professions must decline.

There are numerous examples in the modern world of slip-shod, untrained thought, or lack of it, at work with disastrous results, one reason for the rise in vandalism, the return to the barbaric. If one reveres the craftsmanship of the past, tries to preserve the best of art, architecture and noble idealism of the few great Teachers who have come to live amongst us for a brief while, one surely wonders whether society has really gone a long way from the early primitive conditions when, we are informed by the aid of scientific instruments, life was very much nearer to an animal existence. Such culture that has come down to modern civilisation has so far baffled the modern scientist — the construction of the pyramids, Stonehenge, the many superb examples of design and craftsmanship in wood, metal or cloth . . . all this is ART. It can no more be separated than the worship of God can be kept solely for Sundays.

This is no place to discourse upon morality, but a society that cares so little and punishes so mildly the frequent cases of horrific assault and subhuman behaviour, calls for a new artistic approach to such conduct. Of course when I left the Slade, my intentions were quite clear and I was completely innocent. For proof of this, and you must take my word for it, I only learnt the meaning of the word homosexual at the age of fifty-three!

It seems incredible today but it is true, yet I was well read and, I thought, well-educated. Certain stories that seemed a little puzzling were obviously understood by my friends who evidently thought it unwise to enlighten me.

Not until after my father died did I experience the first and future disgust at having a so-called 'dirty week-end' with a lady twice my age. I told my mother all the appropriate lies for which I have never ever forgiven myself and never, in that sense, repeated. I only state a fact that, today, seems unbelievable.

It is said that "to the pure, all things are impure". Hence it is to me very important that purity and its sister innocence go hand in hand and this is inevitably — and I stress the word 'inevitably' — reflected in one's work which is, after all, always a self-portrait. It is important to understand this for man is a natural cheat and so is woman; it is because of crudity, greed, pretence... The rather tired old saying that God is not mocked is unfortunately as true today as when it was first uttered, also that "Like attracts like". What has all this to do with art? It is ART. Art is the opportunity, like writing, to see ourselves as we truly are and that is the sole purpose, not only of art but of everything mankind does while he, or she, exists on this earth.

. . . .

So art is not a thing apart as so many ignorant people would have us believe; it is the soul trying to rise above the animal. Art is everywhere for the trained eye to observe. Of course I realise that I must confine myself to drawing and painting because that is what my proposed book is all about.

There is no attempt to teach others. All I want is to try to hand over for a brief while the bifocals I have so painfully acquired especially as a student at the Slade where I went by the courtesy, love and generosity of a father, my beloved father, who saw in his son sufficient talent and ability to love art in all its varied aspects along with the tenacity and high-mindedness that can only belong to youth, to embolden him to take me to the best Art School of the time.

My three years at such a romantic place as the Slade were filled with the joy of work. I also came, very shyly, into the company of other students, male only, as the sexes were kept separate except in the anatomical room where we did mingle a little. The fact of my being so young kept up my fantastic ignorance and art became the passion of my life. Being very shy, a somewhat immature shabby little boy (for I was very small), I was grateful to artists like Stanley Spencer who had come for a refresher course and who went out of his way to be kind to me as a person — more than could be said for the élite, the winners of the *Prix de Rome* and favoured of the masters as might be expected. I never had a real talent, not the Augustus John sort which was so self-evident in the few framed drawings that the Slade proudly display as examples to students to be inspired by and to emulate.

. . . .

I never had any painting lessons at the Slade as my father detested the New English Art Club attitude that prevailed in my time — the 'twenties — saying that the teaching of painting was thoroughly bad. The filthy colour and the construction of what passed for a painting seemed to him a bad joke and certainly a bad example to his son who had copied the works of the Brabazon School, Diaz, Corot, Millet, Rousseau, Daubingy and many others.

I also copied the works of John Constable, Frank Brangwyn, Henrietta Bonner,

Anna Airey, Sir Alfred Munnings, George Stubbs, J.F. Ferneley and so many others including the Koek-Koek School, then known in dealer's circles as the Teatray School. Then there were the works of Fantin-Latour and James Whistler, in fact and indeed any type of painting that came my father's way in his business. He had a theory that the old traditional method of copying which had been practised until the advent of the French Impressionists (who broke with all art training and tradition) was the original inspiration of many of the great artists. I copied many of the 17th century Dutch artists, the down-to-earth, fantastic ability of these Masters impressed a young, aspiring artist very deeply. Even now, when my life is drawing to its inevitable end, I see how this versatility I undoubtedly possess has had two curious effects. Firstly, it has enabled me to survive — I always think of the great Talleyrand's sardonic reply as to what he did in the French Revolution — "I survived!"

Secondly, I have never had to teach or write or tell anybody how to learn to paint or draw. Many have asked me, of course, and my reply has always been: "Don't. But if you must, just splash about and enjoy yourself."

I can say this, indeed I will say this, that in all the hellish struggles I have had in this horrible incarnation I was foolish enough to have to endure (in spite of all the love of my parents and the many talented, extremely kind artists I have met throughout my long life), I never again want to become an artist. It has brought me in contact with the worst as well as the best in the people I have inevitably met.

I can truthfully say that to have to earn a living by the profession of art is as disillusioning as Mozart, dying at a very early age, is reputed to have said, "Don't take up the study of music; there's no money in it." I, too, quite frankly say that I have been as cruelly exploited in my long years of innocence, exploited by those who only saw in my work an easy way of making what the Americans call 'a fast buck'.

I have learned some amazing lessons. I have learned that man can rise from the dark filth of the earth into which he must be born, rise like the lotus flower up through the murky depths until the bud reaches the surface and there opens, spotless in its purity, to receive the Light and start its journey. That simile, which artistically naturally appeals to me, can be found in all teachings. One nearer to my limited comprehension is that of the young Albrecht Dürer who wrote that if the student would give his whole devotion to the study of Nature, Nature would ultimately reward him with an entirely new vision. The depth of this observation is not at first very obvious; it takes aeons of time with buckets of tears and anguish of spirit fully to understand such wisdom. Only now can I dimly see that, until the artist can and will use this purity and devotion, his soul will not be released from its human bondage. Our desires drag us down to earth — but it takes a great soul to realise this.

Yet one only has to hold a humble acorn in one's hand or, better still, cut it open and try to meditate on the vast lesson that lies there. The acorn contains within itself the huge oak tree which in itself contains the millions of acorns that will grow on its branches, flower, and drop to earth to be reborn in another place there to become an oak tree in its own right. This I have at last learned after seventy-three years of practicing the profession of Art.

I know, too, that this applies to every human being, call them male or female;

it is the Law, the Law that needs no Courts of Justice, no figures holding swords or scales. It is the message of a Higher Power, a Power we gullibly hope to cheat. But man cannot make the acorn or the possibilities that lie within it. This should, but will not, be taught to every child as he leaves off his toys and lays down the hammers, swords, bombs or any of the false doctrines he loves to invent.

Art is seeing, and seeing truly, for a purpose; that our art galleries are enriched by the efforts of paint on canvas is just a by-product for which we should be duly grateful but an earthquake or fire can obliterate all traces in a short space of time. What cannot be obliterated is what mankind can learn from it, 'it' being his or her puny little moment of earthly existence. I can do no better than end this chapter, indeed the book, with the words:

Be not deceived, God is not mocked. ''As a man sows, so shall he reap also'', down to the last jot and tittle, and that applies to EVERYONE. That, to me, is the *raison d'être.*

The End

Editor's note: This rather strange chapter tells little of Vernon's life immediately following his years at the Slade although there are brief references in other writings to the time between the Slade and his father's death, in 1926, which cut him deeply. Vernon has concluded this chapter as 'End of Book', as he has made abundantly clear, his whole life was his Edwardian childhood, the rest an existence hardly worth recording. Again, this was written wearing the rose-tinted spectacles through which he always saw his childhood and before the bitterness of age and illness took over. Life was not all bad as his ample correspondence indicates and the tributes from his friends and associates bear out.

While there was always a dark side to Vernon's character, towards the end of his life there set in an increasing bitterness against the fate that had decreed, despite his perfect background and privileged training, that he was not to become what he termed ''a real artist''. When he was stricken with severe arthritis, this dark side of his nature rather took over and some of his writings betray a resentment towards life that had, for many years, been kept under control to the extent that he had earned for himself the reputation of ''a painter of sweetness and light''.

Much of his bitterness and cynicism was unwarranted for seldom has an artist become such a household name in his own lifetime. Vernon might argue that, this having been achieved largely through the denigrated medium of 'commercial art', was meaningless but not so. As the standard of reproduction of quality prints and greeting cards has dramatically improved, the 'cheap' prints have been forgotten and the advertisements and book illustrations are virtually unknown to the hundreds of people who have derived tremendous pleasure from good Vernon Ward prints and now, already, his original works are much sought after and commanding high prices. Many of the great artists had to earn their crust through commercial art but posterity has an uncanny way of sorting the sheep from the goats and immortalising those whose work deserves to live for ever.

. . . .

After leaving the Slade, Vernon joined his father in the business, at the same time continuing to paint and draw for himself as much as time allowed and to frequent museums and art galleries, absorbing like a sponge all he could learn about art and artists.

Even restoration fascinated him: ''I remember getting a large old canvas for sixpence, rolled up, dark brown, with thirty-two holes in it! It had a 'feel' about it, though, a feel that it had once been a reasonably decent old painting. I had it relined, then cleaned it and stopped up the holes, finding under the darkened varnish and dirt, a tolerably good Dutch 17th century shipping scene. I used to restore it, a little at a time, in my spare time, and after a period of about two years, there was a very nice picture. There was a lot of 'new' paint on it but some dealer was pleased to give me £60 for it — I felt absurdly pleased that I had rescued some unknown Dutch artist from oblivion.''

Around this time, Albert Ward took his son to Bruges, a lovely city thankfully unscathed from the recent war: ''That beautiful city was still uninfested by the motor-car. To those who will never see what I saw, never know the types of people I saw and sketched, the old women making lace sitting outside their age-old homes, Flemish like their ancestors who had lived and died in the city of Bruges, never see the dogs drawing little carts or watch the long narrow carts, so picturesque, that can be seen in the seventeenth century Dutch pictures. They seemed almost unchanged since Brueghel, van Ostade, Teniers and many others painted those that can be seen in our National Gallery or Apsley House, Hyde Park.

''Oh, the very memory of old Bruges before the tourist and phony-ness that tourism inevitably brings! I write of Bruges, the Venice of the North, with its lovely old charm before exploitation.

''One lovely sunny morning we went on a tour of the battlefields. There, near Ypres, I stood on the top of a trench and looked down on rusting old tanks lying like drunken prehistoric monsters on the shell-holed road. The black stumps of trees stood by, lonely and horrible.

''The trenches zig-zagged in strange cuttings in this strange dead landscape, smashed farmhouses, the beautiful tower of Ypres Town Hall, where snipers shot and killed the unwary, lying in a heap of rubble, ghosts of dead men that seemed to haunt the newly growing grass while at my feet was a clump of scarlet poppies, their frail blood-red petals waving in the summer wind. I stared and stared. So this was where so many fine young men fought and stabbed at other fine young men in greeny grey uniforms, men who came back shell-shocked, men who were ordered to stand to the last man...

"I thought of our shop boy who lied about his age, coming running into the shop. Matthew was his name and we all loved him. 'Good-bye, Guv'nor, Ma'am,' he said, his fine sturdy figure in puttees, huge boots and a rifle that seemed gigantic. 'It'll be over by Christmas and I'll be back.'

"Ah, poor Mat. Six weeks hurried training at Aldershot, a couple of days leave and then, almost unbelievably, came the yellow telegram — Private Matthew XYZ, killed in action. His Majesty regrets. . .

"My mother burst into tears and cried as only a woman can. It brought home to us all the grim reality of war, accentuated as I stood, the Flanders poppies at my feet, looking at the rotting sandbags, the escaping sand looking like some ghastly blood from another planet. Still younger than Matthew, tears pricked my eyes. . ."

. . . .

Albert Ward's health was already beginning to deteriorate when Vernon left the Slade. The struggle for survival with the attendant strain and worry of the war years when he had run his business almost single handed, his wife taking paying guests to help the meagre income, had taken its toll along with the driving, remorseless energy that always consumed him. By the time Vernon was approaching his twenty-first birthday, his father was a physical wreck, unable to sleep for persistent coughing and losing strength rapidly. A specialist was called in and, somehow, the Wards raised enough money to send him to Switzerland. Sadly, it was too late and after only two months he died in the sanatorium in Leysin.

Encouraged by regular letters from his father, Vernon had struggled to keep the business going with an occasional illustration or other commission to help their dwindling finances. His mother's paying guests were charged a rather inadequate two guineas a week for bed, breakfast and often an evening meal — all hard earned pennies for which mother and son both worked themselves ceaselessly "to help father", to avoid worrying him with financial problems. Nevertheless, his illness was expensive and, when he died, Vernon and his mother were left almost penniless.

While the grief stricken Mary Ward went to Leysin, Vernon tried his best to continue with the business and to answer the many kind and sympathetic enquiries from friends and customers, feeling all the time that he was living in a strange dream that was totally unreal. Returning in sombre black bringing home her husband's few personal possessions, Mary Ward's indomitable spirit rose to the emergency in which they found themselves. Part of the corner shop premises was sold off to a hairdresser, the rest she divided in two using the 'new' one as a florist's business. She encouraged Vernon to continue with his art work while, in his turn, he helped all he could with her venture, taking her to Covent Garden at six o'clock in the morning to buy fresh flowers. In spite of all their brave efforts, the florist's was not an outstanding success; both were novices at the game and, in the hard post-war years, money for such luxuries as flowers and paintings was hard to come by.

Vernon saw this as the end of his artistic career although I would be inclined to agree with those who see it as a new beginning, certainly a valuable experience. Undoubtedly it was a struggle. No painting pictures for the sheer joy of it but living by drawing and painting commercially ''as I was forced into doing, which resulted in creating ideas, schemes, for greeting cards, pictures for reproduction, ever watchful of the changing fashion which exists in this world as much as fashion changes in clothes, interior décor and the public's attitude which is always being assailed and conditioned by advertising, films, plays, books, records — by big business''.

With hindsight, perhaps it should be gratitude for this rather than bitterness that Vernon felt in his old age. In those hard times when poverty and unemployment were rampant, it would have been hard to survive by painting beautiful works of art to hang, admired but unsold, on gallery walls. Only those artists with the talent and versatility, which Vernon Ward undoubtedly possessed, to turn to commercial work and make a success of it were in a position to indulge their creative abilities to any extent at all without resort to teaching, some menial mechanical work or, worst of all, the dole.

(See colour on page 130.)

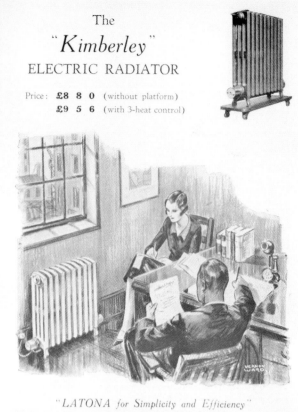

The
"Kimberley"
ELECTRIC RADIATOR

Price: **£8 8 0** (without platform)

£9 5 6 (with 3-heat control)

"LATONA for Simplicity and Efficiency"

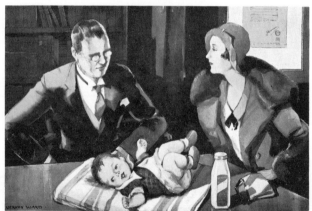

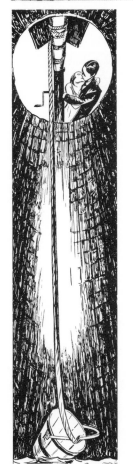

ESCAPING THE BLUES

CONSTANT
HOT WATER
AT A
CONSTANT
TEMPERATURE

World Stories Brought to Life.

From the Painting by De Beauvois Ward.

Cultural Entertainment

THE *foregoing series "World Stories Brought to Life" has illustrated the wide range and variety of subjects covered by Everybody's.*

Literature, Art, Music, Medicine, The Drama, etc. . . . Something to interest everybody's interests; written and illustrated by the foremost authorities. An education with entertainment for all.

MEMORIES OF VERNON

As far as Vernon's own autobiographical reminiscences are concerned, there is a yawning gap between the death of his father in 1926 and the meditations of his old age when the whole of his life was discoloured by the crippling arthritis that no longer allowed him to paint.

Always a prolific letter writer, digressing into deep philosophies even in business letters when some chance reference triggered off another train of thought, his correspondence provides a further valuable character study. Always, too, one senses the undoubted truth that Vernon himself had little interest in writing of his adult life for posterity; nostalgia for his Edwardian childhood became more obsessive as he grew older and it was on these years that he looked back through a golden, sunlit haze.

As a painter, Vernon Ward was known to a much wider public than many of his artist contemporaries. The sad fact is that far too many people know of him through indifferent reproductions with which familiarity bred contempt. It might have been some consolation to him to remember that one of East Anglia's greatest artists, John Constable himself, is identified even today in the minds of many by totally distorted reproductions of such subjects as 'The Hay Wain' obtainable free with x number of packet tops!

The need to earn a living at such an early age and the overexposure that inevitably resulted, has undoubtedly prevented too many genuine art lovers from gaining an awareness of the true quality of his work. It was always a sore point with him, quite naturally, that certain galleries refused to promote his work because of the impression created by his so-called 'commercialism'. Having said that, as the standard of reproduction improved immeasurably and as Vernon forsook the 'cheaper' end of advertising and illustrative work, concentrating his painting for reproduction on very high quality prints and greeting cards, there are many who have had second thoughts about this 'commercial art' and have set out to learn more of his original work and discover its whereabouts.

Later in his life some extremely prestigious commissions came his way and paintings were purchased by serious collectors and connoisseurs and for influential presentations. His Exhibitions at the King Street Galleries, as Noël Napier-Ford tells us, were highly successful, leading to others up and down the country and eliciting from Vernon himself the admission that, at last, he was becoming the artist he was always meant to be.

To return to his earlier years, many kind people have contributed their memories of Vernon and his work and helped me to fill the gaps in his own reminiscences. Noël Syers, himself an artist, one time art editor of *Everybody's* and, in his time, a prominent figure in the art world, probably remembers Vernon's early life better than anyone else alive today.

First Meeting with Vernon Ward

by Noël Syers   March 1986

Having met Bert Fiddes Watt at Goldsmiths' College as a student, being interested in psychic matters he took me to a lecture on Reincarnation at a lady's flat opposite the Natural History Museum in South Kensington.

Sitting beside me was a small, dark, very alert Scotsman who was very interested in these lectures by Mr. Wyeth and Mr. Meale who revealed an extraordinary knowledge of occult matters. Mr. Meale (an ex tram driver) claimed to be a seer and *did* give extraordinary diagnoses which were confirmed by several doctors who were interested.

When in course of conversation, I told the gentleman (Howard Elcock, artist and illustrator for the *Sketch, Sphere* and *Tatler*) that my studio was decorated like a Tunisian Café from where I had just returned, he told me that *his* studio was in the Arab style, on top of Haverstock Hill, Hampstead. Would I like to see it as he was shortly going to America?

It turned out to be the luxurious studio of Carl Haag, a well known and respected German artist of the 1890s who had worked in Cairo and imported Egyptian wood and plaster-work, tiles and artefacts, to build a complete Arab Egyptian interior! The police (World War I) discovered that his studio with its large skylight was being used by the Germans to signal positions to the Zeppelins. The walls of the studio looked like Arab tiles but concealed cupboards behind which were stored wireless transmitters, torches, cameras and so on. The Germans it was learned used the symbol of a lotus flower to mark where a wireless transmitter was hidden and, on pressing a tile with a lotus pattern, the whole wall swung out revealing a spy storehouse.

A small room in the same house, beneath the studio, was *said* to be a meeting place for Edward VII and some of his mistresses, perhaps including the Countess of Warwick. It was quite a small room containing a fine American type four-poster bed with a muslin arch on top. I cannot confirm that this really was so but Howard Elcock said he had been told that when the house was evacuated and he was allowed to leave the studio.

Standing at Howard Elcock's easel was a young art student whom he introduced as someone who wanted to earn money at art. He would try and show us both the right attitude and help us as far as he could before he left. He did, in a few days, give us the essential outlook and within a week he had completely scrapped anything I had learnt at Goldsmiths'!

I invited Vernon to my mother's flat in Bramham Gardens, South Kensington, and we soon became close friends, attending many of Wyeth's lectures on Reincarnation and sessions of healing with 'life force' at the enormous studio of the well known portrait painter, Fiddes-Watt from Aberdeen. This was in Marloes Road and it has since been turned into a hotel with eighteen bedrooms! It had originally been used by a sculptor painter who worked on a large scale.

Vernon's house in South Hill Park Gardens, Hampstead, was full of art studies painted under the direction of his father who had an antique shop opposite Hampstead Heath Station. Most were very accurate copies of assorted, well known pictures; it was the method used at that time. Vernon had also trained at the Slade School under Professor Tonks.

At the time I had just started commercial work having seen a small Exhibition in Bond Street under a famous woman photographer's. A Miss Sharman who was in charge showed me the work of a young artist she had discovered and floated, the now famous Rowland Hilder, but he worked in a very specialised way only. Could Vernon (whose work I had shown her) do some work for her? At that time he was quite sure that he was the reincarnation of the period of the Three Musketeers and had done paintings of them by the dozen.

One I showed her was of two musketeers drinking at a table but when Miss Sharman pointed to the fact that both were almost identical faces (it was the same model, his brother Kyrle drawn from left and right) I was, fortunately, inspired to explain that the painting was called 'The Twins!' She sold it and quite a few more.

When I first met Vernon his colouring was very restrained and dull whilst I was used to the over bright colours of the Tunisian Bazaars and the décor of Diaghilev's Ballet who were living in the flat above ours. It took years for his colours to strengthen and then it was because he was working for Solomon J. Solomon, painting flower pictures. He was goaded into it by bad printing, a misfortune he never quite got away from.

After Howard Elcock had left for New York, Vernon worked quite a bit at Mrs Elcock's flat. At home he was quite the ugly duckling, being totally different to his brothers. Kyrle and Eric sometimes acted as models for him and recognisably appeared in the London street cries. Mrs Elcock's flat was very skilfully decorated in Tudor fashion, black beams and rustic ironwork belonging, I think, to an uncle. There were some very fine pistols, Cromwellian swords and ironwork that would be extremely costly today but were not then thought of as valuable.

I took quite a few photos of Cleo, as she was called, with my mother's old Lancaster quarter-plate camera with a cap, one that she had used in Cairo and on the Nile during the building of the first Aswan Dam which necessitated making the plate in the dark room, a portable sentry box lined with shantung silk! It is still, today, taking very clear and reliable photos.

The photos I took showed Vernon wearing a wig from Clarksons while he imagined the figures in his pictures; he never copied anything exactly, though, but always with his 'feeling' of it. At this time (about 1929), I had one evening just come from Baird's house nearby where he was experimenting with his first television set. It looked like a vaulting horse and on the end appeared a picture reflecting light on a mirror drum — postcard size! I was deeply impressed as he phoned down to the B.B.C. and, as he directed objects to be placed about the stage, they were moved by a stage hand and I *saw* his orders in Hampstead being instantaneously carried out from opposite the Queen's Hall, Lancaster Place, at the end of Regent Street. This was the beginning of television but I never dreamt of the quick evolution into three dimensional colour video of exquisite quality that I should live to see.

On my way back I called at Cleo's place where Vernon was working and found a strange scene — Cleo sitting on a sofa with Vernon lying with his head on a pillow on her lap, apparently in a trance!

In a dreamlike voice he was describing in detail, very vividly, a swordfight between musketeers in an autumn wood, ending up with his wiping the blood off his rapier with a handful of dried leaves...

He 'came to' without remembering anything he had said! It is a strange coincidence that in later life, just before arthritis crippled him, when it was necessary for him to have a steering assisted car to commute between Hampstead and Twickenham, he took up fencing lessons with a fencing tutor near the Cambridge Theatre.

We were both illustrating novels for the publishers, Nelson, at the same time. I was trying to cope with H.G. Wells' 'In the Days of the Comet' and 'Mr. Britling sees it Through', which was biographical, and Vernon had two by another author, I think Jane Austen.

"...the photos I took showed Vernon wearing a wig..."

We were very close friends. His mother was turning their old antique shop into a florist's as things were a bit difficult and Vernon used to drive her to Covent Garden market at 4 o'clock in the morning to obtain a stock of flowers. It must have been a strain although he was very athletic then; he used to ride a motor bike to Wales where he loved painting the hills, a subject of which he would have liked to paint 'academy' pictures had not necessity forced him into commercial art.

I remember having great fun at South Hill Park Gardens converting the conservatory into a kitchen when they divided the house into flats — a real art deco of the twenties! His brother Cyril was working at Rowleys, a marvellous art shop in Kensington Church Street where they manufactured exquisite frames, panelling and furniture coloured in a mixture of gold and warm silver, also parchment lampshades (a novelty then) and hand-made pottery with jugs of blue thistles and 'honesty' leaves. A favourite still-life of the period!

At that time we could not even imagine meetings with Sir William Russell Flint when each admired the other's art — Sir William's delightful watercolour nudes and Vernon's exquisite flowers. I remember helping Vernon to arrange the first flower window display at their old shop.

The centre piece was a Chinese garden with a three foot Chinese porcelain pagoda constructed to show several waterfalls on the way down after water had been poured in the reservoir at the top. I gave Vernon a small electric pump which I had used in a fountain in the middle of my studio at Bramham Gate. People would not bother to go round it but would step over it, sunk in the floor, which ended in so many wet feet that I removed it.

In those days we had many, most interesting, conversations with all sorts of people, lying around on divans in my Arab room in which we 'talked the earth off its axis'. There were, too, many visits to art galleries and the Victoria and Albert Museum where we discovered a fairyland of beauty that helped to form our taste. It was a quite enchanting time, discovering both art and ourselves, and although we had very separate tastes, we had an extraordinary ability to enjoy the same things. I was able to introduce Vernon to a new world and he introduced me to a much more mature outlook.

I would very much have liked my two closest friends, Vernon Ward and Fiddes Watt, to become friends also but they just could not harmonise. Fiddes and I were interested in the Caledonian Market every Friday and Vernon in the National Gallery. (This remark is meant to be partly metaphorical!)

While Vernon was painting all sorts of genre pictures for Solomon and Whitehead, I laboured on the lowly form of book jackets. As a moral supporter and ally, Vernon was invaluable as our ideas seemed to supplement each other. At that time John Murray's were publishing P.C. Wren's *Beau Geste* novels with great success and, when their illustrator became an alcoholic, they contacted me as the only artist they knew who was familiar with North Africa and the Foreign Legion. Could I let them have a finished book jacket within twenty-four hours as it was due at the printers the next day?

I worked right through the night while Vernon fortified me with plenty of black coffee, then he delivered the design for me the next morning. It appeared as an advertisement on the buses as well as on the book jacket and led to a long succession of different editions of P.C. Wren's works which brought me into interesting personal contact with the author.

Then came the upheaval of the war. I had moved to a Victorian house in Chippenham, both Vernon and I were out of work and neither of us much liked the idea of enlisting in the army. I found a 'safe' job with Twickenham A.R.P. and Vernon managed to get a job in charge of the maintenance of ambulances at the Air Raid Precautions Depot at Richmond. As this was just on top of Richmond Hill across the river, commuting to Hampstead was impossible so he came to stay with me. As everyone who could had evacuated from London, the flat below mine was empty so Peter Parrot, who helped Vernon and I with our accounts, moved in. His daughter became a 'Bluebell Dancer' at the *Folies Bergère* and an entirely new phase came into our lives.

During the 'phoney war' period when nothing in the way of expected air-raids was happening, Vernon painted an over lifesize pastel of Marianne, the symbol of France, as a backdrop for some shows at the Friarstyle Depot. I never saw these

98

but we both entered pictures for an Exhibition of A.R.P. artists held in Bond Street. Vernon's were of battle scenes with Marianne leading and mine were of first aid post incidents; one which was painted with watercolour mixed with Pears transparent soap to look like oils on a sandbag ground, captured the imagination of the Press and was sold before the show was opened by Colonel Lovelace.

At one stage in the war, Vernon was stationed at a lovely old Georgian house in Petersham (now occupied by Tommy Steele) where he painted a number of garden studies and a large oil painting of searchlights picking up German bombers over Petersham Golf Club — entirely in black and white. I remember, too, a small sketch of some of the old oaks there, their leaves blown back by the wind against a stormy sky which was one of Vernon's own favourite paintings. In a small but heavy gilt frame, it would have passed for a Constable and was most impressive. Perhaps it was the outcome of the many sky studies from his bedroom at the top of South Hill Park Gardens where he spent many hours trying to paint skies like Constable. He succeeded . . .

During the war we used to listen in great admiration to J.B. Priestley's talks on the wireless for he seemed to express so well our own sentiments. We were very patriotic and, when peace was declared, we celebrated at our table in the conservatory in full evening dress using our best glass and china for our corned beef sandwiches!

It was about this time that I first noticed Vernon having muscular spasms of the spine when sleeping; he would suddenly spring off, his back in an arc.

Another thing I remember during the war was Vernon planning in great detail a painting of Chopin giving a recital before a distinguished audience. The study of the Princess d'Agoult as hostess used to hang over our mantelpiece in a fine Hogarth frame in mahogany and gold and I still think this is one of the finest paintings he ever did. He admired Chopin tremendously and always had a vase of violets on the table in memory of him, though I never remember him playing Chopin records or listening to his music on the wireless. He always had music playing while he was painting but so softly that, to me, it was simply a blur of sound.

He had Howard Elcock's easel standing in the bow window in a north east light and used an old dumb waiter, partly to accommodate all his tubes of paint, bottles of medium and suchlike, and partly as a palette which was always oiled and cleaned with loving care. He used an extraordinary range of brushes sometimes laying in the background of skies with a large housepainter's brush. His favourite medium was poppy oil, used very sparingly, and he finished with copal varnish. Always he signed his work well before finishing, regarding this as part of the painting's composition.*

He always sketched directly from life in pencil or charcoal sometimes adding watercolour to make as careful a study as many artists would consider a finished painting. He never let this inhibit him though, and I have known him scrape out whole passages with a razor blade, sometimes some of the finest areas if he considered them 'purple passages' that would spoil the whole concept. Sometimes five or six passages would be scraped out and painted over but there was no indication of this in his finished work; he gloried in the physical manipulation especially with great blobs of impasto being brought under control on the canvas.

Vernon was a great believer in regular hours of work and even if not 'inspired' would work until he was. He was very conservative in his use of colour. I introduced him to some very subtle Belgian and French colours thinking their delicacy and transparency would be useful for his beautiful flower paintings but I never saw him use them. He simply said that thirty six shades of grey were sufficient for him, one of his favourites I remember was made from emerald green and rose madder.

. . . .

* The importance of the signature as an integral part of the composition is characteristic of Professor Tonks' pupils. I have met this several times and could wish that more present day teachers followed his example!   J.W.

Portrait of the Countess of d'Agoult

In attempting to bring in to one comprehensive group the friends and admirers of Frederick Chopin, I had to recourse to all the books I could find relating to such a distinguished assembly. Many portraits of Chopin's admirers I was able to copy but, in spite of exhaustive research, I could not find any real portrait of the Countess. To gather such well-known companions in the 'Life of Chopin' I decided to recreate in 1946/7 the verbal portraits I had read about the Countess d'Agoult.

It was said that she and the composer Franz Liszt were much in love and that he brought her over after he had emerged from years of retirement when he was known as the Abbé Liszt and they stayed in an apartment confronting the magnificent view of the Thames from Richmond Terrace. She stayed there while Liszt accepted an invitation to see Queen Victoria and the Prince Consort, both great music lovers.

The picture, in the costume of the period, must stand therefore as the artist's idea of how this aristocratic lady might possibly have been observed listening to Chopin, so soon to die surrounded by countless admirers.   *Vernon Ward.*

'Chopin playing to his friends 1843'.

If there is a certain amusing 'grasshopper' tendency about Noël Syers' reminiscences (for I have tried not to edit out of character), it must be remembered that he is now an old man and it is quite remarkable that his memory should be so clear. For the record, too, perhaps I should mention that, at eighty-six, he is still very much the commercial artist, working away at his designs and illustrations despite being confined to a wheel-chair which he skilfully manipulates to position himself and his work just where he wants them to be.

There are other notes, fragmentary memories jotted down as they occurred to him. Some I feel, are worth recording as they came, as part of the jig-saw make up of Vernon Ward.

"Physically, though small, he was a graceful mover with a strong sense of rhythm, good at skating, swimming, fencing and dancing though, sadly, he never seemed to find a dancing partner his own size. Always he looked his best in full evening dress being particular about line and immaculate cut, and he danced superbly with Cleo Elcock and Mrs Savours, a great personal friend who, with her brother, had been a professional dancer. They made a graceful couple dancing

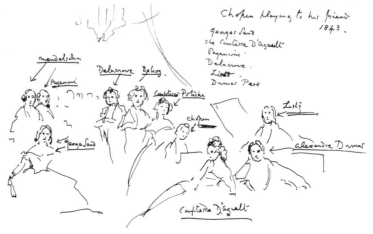

together but one was always aware of her looking down on top of his head which, as in the case of many clever men, acquired a 'polish' quite early. Nevertheless, with his massive, thoughtful cranium this almost became an adornment!

"Together we made many delightful forays to photograph the swans from Richmond Bridge and the deer in the Park. Long walks along the tow-path beneath the bridge produced many charming pictures of ducks with baby ducklings scuttling along behind, one chick less each day with a fearful mortality of which the mothers seemed quite careless. Fleets of elegant white birds gliding under the sunlit arch of the bridge and floating through the mist provided inspiration for future paintings which became very popular as full sized art prints, still hanging in homes all over the world.

Reproduced by courtesy of W.R. Royle Ltd.

"It was the film 'Bambi' that first attracted him to deer and I took many photographs of him feeding them near the White House in Richmond Park where Edward VIII was born. The house is now a ballet school which gave him ideas for many dancing subjects, meticulously researched and worked up from beautifully detailed pastel sketches almost inspired by Degas. Vernon's had a much more feminine feel with a mystical shimmer of blues, greys and silver, but, somehow, he never achieved quite the sense of movement he wished to convey.

"Saturday lunches at the Swiss café, endless deep and interesting discussions, timeless moments strolling on the terrace by the river, feeding swans, staggered by the sight of the enormous laburnams in bloom, with their cascades of golden blossom, the magnificent fountain with groups of sea-nymphs with its magical effect in certain lights. . . . all these are memories of Vernon. Another delight of these weekend excursions was the simultaneous recognition of the artistic beauties of line and texture and the perfect calm, despite the war, of these gardens drenched with the heady perfume of roses. The charm of Vernon's sensitive personality and the great knowledge and thoughtful analysis that chrystalized my own thoughts is something I shall always be grateful for.

"Vernon travelled a great deal and painted in many countries. He loved to entertain his friends in France being proud of his de Beauvoir ancestry — he used the name, too, when signing paintings he was particularly pleased with. We spent an unforgettable holiday in Venice, where he had previously been with his father, and revelled in the sheer beauty and the wonderful art treasures. I don't remember him doing any sketches himself — perhaps they had all been done too many times before!"

Another friend who shared Vernon's war was Laura Dance, still living in Richmond, who writes of what she terms the Civil Defence period. Perhaps unfortunately, she focuses rather more on the so-called 'phoney war' than the real thing in which I believe Vernon acquitted himself very bravely.

From Laura Dance, Richmond, November 1986

I must first have met Vernon in the winter of 1940, just after my eighteenth birthday although I have no real recollection of our first meeting. I met my future husband about the same time and, to this day, every detail of that meeting is engraved on my mind; with Vernon it was different, he just seems always to have been around and part of my life.

We were both given jobs in the local A.R.P., later to have the somewhat grander name of Civil Defence. I was supposedly an ambulance attendant. I'm not sure what Vernon was but we were stationed with stretcher bearers and heavy rescue teams made up mainly of local tradesmen, fishmongers, dustmen and so on but, with no air raids in the early stages of the war, we had rather a lot of time on our hands. Vernon taught me to drive and to play chess and we would talk (or rather, he would!) for hours on end, mainly about religion and all sorts of obscure subjects. I imagine he was a fairly well known artist even then but this I did not realise. To me he was an elderly gentleman, about thirty-five, taking a kindly interest in a somewhat naïve eighteen year old.

Later in that year we were moved *en masse* to the Richmond Golf Club (much to the annoyance of the genuine members), a lovely Georgian building surrounded by golf links and trees, and it was there that I came to know him really well. The thing I remember most was the fun we had chasing each other to work on our bicycles called, for some reason or other, Strawberry and Blackberry, dodging the cars and buses and eventually arriving at our destination. He gave me the name of 'Troggy' (troglodyte) but whether or not that was a compliment I'm not quite sure!

We spent our days pretending to clean ambulances, swotting up our first aid and waiting for the air raid sirens. Vernon was usually to be found painting enormous backcloths for future depôt dances, lovely Arcadian scenes, jungles with black panthers waiting to pounce, Pan playing his pipes and one special one of the personnel in caricature. There were long intense conversations with Vernon holding court surrounded by depôt ladies from various social backgrounds. In theory we were all engaged for some purpose on the same level but social prejudice dies hard and a few of the senior ladies, whose previous contact with dustmen had probably been limited to handing over a gratuity at Christmas, were over the moon to find a well known artist, and an extremely interesting man to boot, with whom to while away the long 'on duty' hours.

This, then, was our war. We seemed to live in a somewhat secluded world all of our own and I remember it, as I know Vernon did, as a happy world far away from the ghastly apparatus of war.

'Summer Fragrance'
"...one could smell the flowers..."

Reproduced by courtesy of W.R. Royle Ltd.

Time does not stand still, however, and with the end of the war our paths separated, Strawberry and Blackberry were put out to grass and we went our own ways without ever entirely losing touch. I married and brought up a family while Vernon went on painting, painting and painting. His cards were in every shop window, his pictures were in every hotel room, and with the general public he was becoming more and more popular. He was to the art world what Ivor Novello was to music and the theatre; his paintings were so lovely, one could smell the flowers, see the butterflies wings in motion, hear the cries of the seagulls and breathe the tang of the sea. He appealed to the masses in the same way as Novello's music and never to my knowledge did he paint anything ugly or difficult to understand.

Many people do not realize how prolific he was or how varied his subject matter — flowers, landscapes all over the world, Edwardian and Victorian scenes and conversation pieces, ballet, all forms of illustration and even a few portraits. I have one of myself in what passed as our Civil Defence uniform, armed with a gas mask, tin hat perched on my head. It has always had pride of place in my sitting room and will, I hope, be passed on to my grandchildren as a record of what I and thousands like me did during the Second World War.

Years later our paths crossed again and we resumed something of our old friendship but it was a changed Vernon I found. The sparkle and fun were still there but to a much lesser degree having been largely replaced by bitterness and a cynical approach to life; the arthritis which was poisoning his body was having a similar effect on his mind, and who can wonder? The one thing in life that he loved above everything else was being wrested from him; he was still struggling to paint but his poor crippled hands could hardly hold a brush and he was no longer able to stand at his easel.

It was with great sadness that I learnt of his death in a nursing home in 1985. He had been part of my life for forty years and there were many memories that I treasured, yet mingled with the sadness, was relief and gratitude that suffering was with him no longer. The world has lost a good, maybe great, artist and I will always mourn the loss of a dear friend.

Laura Dance in Civil Defence uniform, 1940.

"...even from Marrakesh!"   *Reproduced by courtesy of W.R. Royle Ltd.*

'BECKY'

The person who knew him best of all and was his companion, help and very loyal friend for nearly forty years was 'Becky' (another Vernon nickname) Groombridge at whose instigation this book is being compiled.

Becky first made Vernon's acquaintance about the same time as Laura Dance and, later, as well as becoming his secretary and personal assistant her husband became his accountant and close friend. Both were a tremendous help to Vernon in many, many ways, particularly Becky who, both before and after her husband's death, devoted her life to Vernon, seeing him through a distressing nervous breakdown and, later, through his last illness preceded by the years of cynicsm and depression brought on largely by the crippling arthritis which was destroying his lifeline — the ability to paint. Ironically, after his school experiences and the lasting impression they left, he died in Twyford Abbey, a big monastery-like nursing home run by the Alexian Brothers.

Mary Ward 1950.

Becky has talked to me a great deal about Vernon, so much that I have, for a long time, felt that I knew him much more closely than our belated correspondence acquaintance, however pleasant, made possible. All the same, I wanted Becky to write some of her own memories for me and for all those admirers of his work who may read this anthology of his life and art. After summarising his early life so extensively recalled by Vernon himself she continues...

Now perhaps I should start again under the heading, 'When I first met Vernon'. At the same time as Laura Dance (our birthdays are within three months of each other), I was transferred from my Civil Defence post in Sudbrook Park, not the depôt she mentions but in the same park, to an ambulance depôt in Friars Stile Road, Richmond. When I arrived feeling very nervous, Vernon was on holiday but all the other girls warned me that he was a devil to work for and I had better beware. Having put the fear of God into me before I even started, very much a new girl torn from my wealthy sheltered background, in desperation and boredom, I started working on the camouflage nets which were put up for us to work on in our spare time!! Then one day a voice whispered in my ear, "He's back", and turning, I saw a small dark haired, quiet man walk into the depôt. He ignored me and went straight to the office, then came out and called, "Miss Ward". I looked round, said "Yes", and followed him into the office.

That was the start of quite an intriguing friendship. He found the similarity in name (Ward) interesting and I found the fact that he was an artist and seemed very lost, equally interesting. I went through much the same experience as Laura but from a different angle. He *was* a lost soul, even in those days, and so was I, so we got on very well. 'Black Crows' on our mutual shoulders were quite a common thing! Slowly, very slowly, he told me the story of his life up till then and I was fascinated, never having met anyone quite like him. I am proud to say now that I helped him with all his wartime posters and his frieze designs for the Ham

Perhaps this is also symbolic of Vernon's own love of flying from 5/- schoolboy 'flips' at Croydon to years of travelling in passenger air liners. In his seventies he still enjoyed watching the little planes at Elstree take off and land; on one memorable occasion he was allowed to fly a school plane on a trial lesson. It took two people to lift him into the plane but he absolutely loved it!

Common Day Nursery — I don't mean on the art side, that was totally his scene, but with the boring bits such as the war poster, 'Wings over Europe', where I painted the map of Europe from the top of a step ladder while he painted the plane.

For some reason Vernon really enjoyed the war — I don't mean the fighting but the fact that his little bit in the war effort seemed to relieve him of all responsibility which, I realised later, meant a lot to him. I shall never forget the day that he went, aged about thirty-six, for his call up interview. He phoned me afterwards with a whoop of glee to say that he was C4 and was to be left in Civil Defence and we went out for a meal to celebrate his release from the prospect of being in the Army. Understandably he had been dreading this from the point of view of damage to his hands.

The war trailed on, eventually the end came and, like Laura, I said, "Goodbye". In 1946 I was seriously ill with double pneumonia and pleurisy which looked like putting paid to my planned skating career; during that period Vernon wrote me several lovely, whimsical letters to try and cheer me up and, eventually, I recovered and started to look for work for myself. My mother, who was very impressed by my friendship with 'the now famous Vernon Ward', suggested that I went to see him at Twickenham where he was sharing the studio with Noël Syer to see if he had any work for me. I went, in fear and trembling, but was welcomed with open arms as he was badly needing a dogsbody to clear up the mess after him and sort out his paperwork and secretarial affairs. I started working for him in 1946 and was with him until his death in 1985; it was a good arrangement for I wanted to pursue my skating career as well and as I was not needed full time, Vernon readily agreed to this.

So, while he was working his way to the top in his field, I was doing the same; I reached my ultimate goal in my field, a Gold Medal for figures and free and a Silver for Ice Dancing, and started judging. This led to a number of trips abroad on both sides of the Iron Curtain, interesting places where I could never have afforded to travel on holiday, and I became a fairly well known International Figure Skating Judge appearing on TV many times to my mother's great delight!

By then Vernon was getting really well known as a 'proper' artist as he called it and, in earning good money, used to spend it just as quickly. Income Tax was a dirty word, he just didn't want to know, but my husband was an accountant so together we tried, not very successfully, to make him see sense. He enjoyed many successful years with plentiful royalties coming in and during the nineteen fifties and sixties was at his peak. For two years running he was the most popular artist on some Radio Programme and his agents were doing very well out of him. They did not have to work at all for their commission, he was so much in demand.

His mother's death in 1962 really broke him up. He suddenly realised that he was responsible for the Hampstead House and the people in it, his job and the flat in Riverdale Road. Briefly this was all too much for him and, coupled with the rheumatoid arthritis that had been with him for several years, caused a complete nervous breakdown. I had to deal with closing down and selling the flat and contents myself; he had had a studio extension built on to the Hampstead house in preparation for the time when he would have to give up Twickenham but, of course, was unable to use it then. A really dreadful seven years followed

One of the frieze designs for the Ham Common Day Nursery.

during which royalties were flooding in and my husband was dealing with his financial affairs with an official account. Fortunately he was able to recommend certain investments which were to prove to be Vernon's lifeline and I dealt with the Hampstead house myself with the help of his long-standing and devoted housekeeper, Annie Salmon.

He returned to Hampstead in 1971 and got down to work again — the start of the very successful period we all know about. One of the highlights of the period was the invitation to paint a 'Swan' picture for a retiring Director of Swan Vesta matches which he much enjoyed. He travelled abroad a good deal at this time which he could well afford to do and almost every trip produced more saleable paintings, even from Marrakesh! Then Knoll House began to feature in his paintings and from there, where he went in May and October for many years, he produced most of his loveliest flower paintings. The Fergusons were extremely kind to him and through them he met many private people who either bought or commissioned paintings from him.

"...one of the highlights of the period..." (see page 113).

At his Chester exhibition with a young admirer.

...and with the Mayor.

Turning to his Exhibitions — I remember three with King Street Galleries, St. James, two at Beckstones Gallery with Kay Jones in the Lake District, one at Chester and one in Derby. The connection with Kay Jones arose from a series of coincidences. My love of Switzerland and my friendship with a Mr. and Mrs Cheasley (skaters) led to Vernon's paying for me to go to Celerina; Cliff Cheasley, a member of the Ealing Art Club, asked me if I thought Vernon would be guest of honour at their Annual General Meeting. To my surprise he agreed and did a very successful demonstration of flower painting; Kay Jones attended this and when she moved North for her husband's health, she opened Beckstones Gallery and asked if Vernon would be their first artist and open the Gallery for them. Again to my surprise, Vernon agreed and with great difficulty I carted him and his pictures up to the Lake District. He was a great success and she has been very successful since, selling the paintings in the North that did not sell so readily in London.

The special features of the Derby Exhibition were his appearance on television which thrilled him and the sale of a watercolour painted in 1924 which he had not intended selling although a woman went, literally, on her knees to him. I said jokingly that he would not sell it for a thousand pounds (a lot of money for a contemporary artist at that time) but she offered him just that and he agreed to sell. Quite a highlight in his life.

I think the decline in Vernon's health and talent that went on from that period is better left unsaid. Through his paintings he lives on in his prime and the painful memories are better buried — there are so many that give joy to us all.

The £1,000 painting — dated 1925.

'The Arcadians'. Becky's own and favourite paintings.   *Reproduced by courtesy of Mrs M.W. Groombridge.*

Becky has made brief mention of Vernon's bi-annual visits to Knoll House, Studland Bay, and the kindness of the proprietors, Col. and Mrs Ferguson. Pauline Ferguson writes —

We first met Vernon in the early sixties soon after my husband and I came to Studland and bought Knoll House Hotel. He had stayed before but it was several years before he returned and this was when we really got to know him; thereafter he came every spring and autumn.

His arrival was always a joy to our permanent staff and ourselves. Becky drove him down from London and would stay herself whenever she could; Vernon always had one of our courtyard suites. On his arrival Norah Wood, our Head Housekeeper would greet him and see that he had all he required including a table for his palette and paints while our porter, Frank Churchill, delighted in arranging everything in its rightful place.

In the dining room Vernon always had a table from which he could look out across the garden with a view of the sea. For dinner he would appear immaculately dressed in dinner jacket and black tie to be greeted by Phyl Gee in the early years and later by Bob Spencer after Phyl retired. There would always be a welcome from our chef, Denis Reavenhall, succeeded by Peter Selby, and from both the under managers — Vernon had arrived at his beloved Studland and second home. He also had many friends among the guests who revisited us at the same time and among the local residents in Studland and Swanage.

To us he was a dear friend, always charming and full of humour and interested in others even at times when we knew him to be suffering pain from arthritis. He loved the spring and the first of the hedgerow flowers and often when out for a

'Violet Time'.
Reproduced by
courtesy of
W.R. Royle Ltd.

Reproduced by courtesy of W.R. Royle Ltd.

Reproduced by courtesy of W.R. Royle Ltd.

drive with Frank Churchill the car would have to stop for him to pick a flower that caught his eye — dog rose, Queen Anne's lace, buttercups or bluebells. Often he would cross the road to stroll on Mary's Ground where wild flowers grew in abundance. He wrote to me:

"Do you know that across the road facing your hotel you have fairy rings of daisies, some tiny wild violets and some very blue bluebells. When the night is lit by a full moon and there is no more sex or violence on television, I creep out into that Fairy Place. The Old Harry Rocks are silent and dim in the moonlight framed by the Pining Pine Trees." Always a romantic!

This is shown by many of his earlier paintings — 'Christmas Parade in Hyde Park', 'Victorian Christmas', and other scenes always of ladies in beautiful crinoline dresses and handsome gentlemen. These paintings show, too, Vernon's knowledge and attention to detail*, his familiarity with the history of costume and architecture and the finer points of birds, dogs and horses. I was fortunate enough to be able to purchase one of his 'Cries of London' series (Peg Woofington, executed in charcoal for which I believe Becky posed) from his Exhibition at the King Street Galleries in May 1977 and I also have 'Gossip in the Park', both of which are a great joy to me.

Once Vernon had settled in the hotel I enjoyed picking flowers for him and many of his most beautiful flower paintings are of those from our garden. I used to take him fresh selections every few days — rhododendron, broom, tulips and daffodils. He loved my Wistaria Floribunda and the longer fall of Wisteria Sinensia. In the autumn the variety was, of course, quite different but, always, his room was full of flowers and we used to run out of vases for he would never let me remove them until the last one had died.

Vernon was very generous and gave me a beautiful oil painting of 'Yellow Dahlias and Butterfly' about which he wrote to me from his home in Hampstead:

"This picture has an ethereal quality and I did not try to work on it; perhaps it will give you the same feeling. Just once in a while the artist paints something for which he can hardly claim authorship — like a magic moonlight it happens and one remembers the moment all one's life. Those moments are rare, like falling in love for the first time!"

Vernon loved Studland and wrote to me in 1977 saying how he wished he had bought a house in the village twenty years before. He wrote in that same letter:

"All my years of holidays at Knoll House and the flowers I have painted from your lovely garden have given pleasure to so many. Age will not wither all I feel for your family and your charming staff. Norah (Wood) is a tower of strength, she blows like a Spring wind along the hotel corridors, hither and thither! You and Ken are lucky to be supported by so many loyal permanent staff and, as my mind turns to your gardens, how lucky to have such able gardeners under Muffy Hobbs."

His letters during the winter months were long and descriptive, often of his Edwardian childhood. To quote from one of these letters — "Once the maids opened the doors to visiting aunts and uncles dressed in their black and white uniforms with little frilly aprons. There was time to stop and something peaceful to stare at and to cross the road was so simple. The railway station at the foot of the road had waiting rooms with a small fire burning in the grate, porters would be sweeping platforms and there were slot machines for Peters and Nestlés chocolate. Slim delights came out of these machines that always worked and were always full. There were 'Ladies' and 'Gentlemen' (not Gents.). The trains puffed in, busy and full of hissing steam with a guard resplendent in gold braid uniform to see long-skirted, be-feathered ladies and silk-hatted gentlemen get in. Doors slammed, the iron monsters emitted a shriek; it growled, hissed and a grimy-faced engine driver pulled a lever and chuff-cher-chuff-chuff. . . With what importance

This is even more remarkable when one realises that practically all Vernon's painting life was achieved with the sight of only one eye, the other having been injured by a tennis ball when he was a very young man.

118

'Gossip in the Park'.

did the guard pocket his watch, roll his green flag and step on to the slowly moving train! All this was so exciting to us sailor-suited boys or pig-tailed (very pullable!), skirted sailor-suited girls in large straw hats. Those peaceful days have long since gone.''

Those letters to me were always so warm and he would write:

''Have a long rest dear Pauline and think of the Spring with the bluebells and buttercups that lie asleep just now. You have a talented husband and two splendid sons and the beautiful, determined Sarah. Soon the Spring will bring me back to dear Knoll House, quite unique, and I delight in telling my friends about such a charming hotel. Your female staff, 'my' artless girls, are a joy to me. I love to see your new season's staff, all so different and so prettily dressed.''

Vernon requested that his ashes should be scattered at Old Harry Rocks* — indeed a sad journey for Becky. So he returned to Studland and the beauty of this village with the seagulls and the return of each season especially the awakening of Spring and the joy he found in painting the flowers he loved with that priceless gift of being able to convey his feelings in all his work.

E.P.F.

Pauline Ferguson,
Studland Bay House, Dorset,
November 1986.

Reproduced by courtesy of W.R. Royle Ltd.

* *In actual fact Vernon had requested that his ashes be scattered on Hampstead Heath as well as Old Harry Rocks and Becky had already complied with this request. When the second time came, she was so overcome by emotion that the ashes were scattered by another very close friend, the actress Joanne Moore.*

'Summer Rhapsody'.   Reproduced by courtesy of W.R. Royle Ltd.

'Symphony in Blue and White'.   Reproduced by courtesy of W.R. Royle Ltd.

As Vernon's own writings clearly indicate, during those bitter and cynical years of his later life, he became quite convinced that he had been the victim of unscrupulous publishers, 'used' to further their own greedy, commercial ends. Undoubtedly in the very early days there may have been a certain amount of truth in this — while 'grubbing around' for outlets, like so many young artists trying to scratch a living, he seized every opportunity to make a few shillings regardless of the reputation of those for whom he worked.

Those days have passed long since although, living as he was in his own past, it may have been the immediate post Slade years that he was subconsciously remembering while his discoloured mental state led him to refer to the entire publishing world as 'a coterie of sharks'.

Working solely for reputable publishers as he did for so many years, there seems to have been a very different relationship to that he suggests. All fine art publishers have a policy to which they adhere and their freelance artists are given ample opportunity to study and agree their contracts. I have been in touch with a number of these people — Sharpes of Bradford (who published his first greeting card subject, 'The Goose Girl', in 1935) the Medici Society, Frost and Reed, Solomon and Whitehead, Royle Publications — directors and staff who remember Vernon personally speak of him with great respect and warmth and have freely offered me their co-operation in providing illustrations for this book or in any other way. Far from being grasping, not one has made a charge for use of copyright, an experience I have rarely encountered.

For many years now we have been pleased to include the works of Vernon Ward amongst our fine art reproductions for the Christmas Season. From his delightful 'Goose Girl', through to the nostalgic church scenes and into his winter landscapes of London's parks, Vernon has proved ever-popular with several generations of card buyers. He lives on through his paintings, which we know will be admired for a long, long time — and we certainly look forward to including his work in many Christmas collections to come.

(A.R. Groves, Art Editor,
Wm. Sharpe Ltd.)

'The Goose Girl, 1935'.

I have been given access to a great deal of correspondence particularly from his major publishers in recent years, Royle Publications, who hold the rights of about 150 subjects:

"My dear Moira," he writes to one of Royles' secretaries, "How sweet of you to write me such a lovely long letter and I am glad you will come to my show.

"Also thank you for suggesting some dates for lunch. Would the 23rd. be good for you (your husband too if he is free) or at a pinch the 30th. October? Let it be Fortnum and Mason's top floor where I'll meet you...

"I hope you don't mind Becky being around — I am in such a state without her help and her car these days..."

There follows six closely written pages, all about the forthcoming Exhibition, back to his childhood and early career, touches of religion and philosophy finishing with "love to Mary and you all."

This is quite typical of many letters to Moira and to Mary Burgess, a former personal secretary of Julian Royle's and a good friend of mine. Julian himself received many such letters — even business correspondence from Vernon to those he really liked was an occasion for a friendly, conversational letter. Writing, for instance, to Julian from Knoll House in the Spring of 1978:

"It is so lovely here after the heavy snow, the wild flowers and ferns, shrubs and trees have all come out together.

"I was just in time to be here in the perfect weather, to see the fields alive and magically spangled with the work of Persephone. The lanes were unbelievable in such frail, tender beauty, impossible to paint, impossible to describe. One can only stand and wonder, with a lifetime of fruitless endeavour, of years spent trying to survive, yet finally rewarded with that new vision that Albrecht Durër wrote of out of his deep spiritual insight. What an artist! Not known half enough in this sadly messed up country.

"How I wish I had studied more deeply these miracles of creation that grow so freely everywhere. By the village there is, in full bloom, a pale pink dog rose bush. The cars hurtle past, canoes, motor boats on trailers, toys to while away the bordeom of being on the lovely beach, the tiny waves rippling in to die with a faint sigh among the sea shells marking the limit of the tide."

Vernon continues philosophising in the way one would talk to a close friend, not a business associate with whom one was battling for rights! Much later in the same letter:

"The publishing world has come into its own and plays a very real part now in the culture of the people. Every card a sermon, every calendar reminding us of change — change, the subtle magician overriding our lives. Change the supreme! As I grow old I look back and see the changes man made or Nature made. Life is delightful or can be and I must get up and dress for breakfast. When I see the shell bay with Bournemouth edging the sea I think of your Father and Mother — they spent their honeymoon here I believe. Dorset is a soft, gentle county, I like to think typically English.

"To love one's land is, in the eyes of a few imbeciles, a wrong thing. 'Racialist' they snarl as if we are not all racialists! Does the cat mate with the dog? What clowns we have in Parliament..."

A few years earlier, in 1974, it had been to Julian Royle he wrote following the dreadful nervous breakdown of which Beck made mention.

"... how I recall telephoning you and saying that I would never paint again! I realise that I owe you and your family, Rowland Hilder and the many others who were so kind and encouraging to me, an attempt at an explanation.

"Due to many causes, some not really capable of any explanation, I had a complete and awful breakdown — of a spiritual, physical and artistic nature. I once told you that I felt I was the artist that never was!!!

"I did and happily now do have some artistic talent which, over the years, I prostituted for money, producing an inner conflict. Other more important things also crowded in and the result was a darkness that bred mental apathy and an unhappiness I did not think possible. Overwork, mental strain... truly a house divided against itself cannot stand!

"Soon I shall have an autumn collection to offer you — ironically some pictures painted before the 'break-up' which I have routed out so that I have BEFORE and AFTER to show you if you are interested. I also have some paintings of wild flowers and hidden in them the happiness of being again able to paint and relive some of my earlier years and there are one or two pictures of the deep love I have of the English landscape with the vigorous skies that my father taught me to observe when we walked over Hampstead Heath together. It is strange to love so much — Victorian assemblies, the lovely moors, the cliffs and green seas of Cornwall, the white gulls, the satin rose and, above all, the beauty of the wild flowers. Having spent these last few years in a dark world, I have come out again to see such beauty... I can scarcely believe the gods could be so kind as to grant me this new vision, this new awareness in a world of unbelievable folly."

And in answer to Julian's reply:

"Your kind and understanding letter gave me such happiness. It is typical of your generous attitude to all things in life to reply so swiftly and react in such a sympathetic manner..."

He closes the letter, again typical of many written to Julian,

"I hope Elizabeth and the boys are flourishing and all the nice people you have at Royle House to whom I send my regards and warm wishes."

The greeting inside the card illustrated suggests that these warm wishes are sincerely reciprocated.

For Vernon from all your many friends and admirers at Royle House

Wishing you a happy Birthday and remembering the happiness your work has brought to millions of people

In his turn, Julian Royle writes of Vernon —

VERNON WARD

I believe the first Vernon Ward painting we bought for publication was entitled 'White Mantle over Dorset' in 1952. It preceded my arrival at the Company by ten years but I was fortunate in meeting Vernon with my parents when we visited his studio.

Vernon was a true romantic. Living alone, his home and studio retained an Edwardian aura which ideally set off his superb period studies of ladies of fashion and their uniformed maids. I felt his love of Dorset and of Studland in particular provided the perfect annual escape to nature where the countryside and the wild flowers and cottage gardens offered a year's inspiration to produce his second love, the painting of flowers. My mother, who is a talented artist, encouraged Vernon on his rare visits to our family home, deep in the Essex countryside, to painting growing flowers rather than formal arrangements in vases and this freer period of Vernon's work in the sixties produced some of his finest works. As a wedding present he gave my wife and I a pair of natural flower studies, one of nasturtiums and one of chrysanthemums, which are treasured by us and continue to delight our family and guests. Needless to say they were successfully reproduced by us as fine art prints and greeting cards together with hundreds of other glorious flower paintings by Vernon.

Vernon was, however, much more passionately interested in figure and costume studies and was totally captivated by the complexities of polite society in the late Victorian and Edwardian period. Many of these studies became the subjects of successful greeting cards which capture the spirit of 'upstairs, downstairs' with remarkable insight.

Reproduced by courtesy of Julian A.C. Royle.

Vernon was a delightful correspondent and I have retained many of his letters some of which include pen sketches of the ladies he is describing with equal ability. His imagination and empathy for the lady's maid reveals his often mentioned wish to be reincarnated as one of these essential props of elaborate Edwardian society. He even had a lady's dummy in his studio dressed with a uniform complete with lace collar, cuffs and apron, such was his conviction that his second coming was to be in this guise.

Vernon was deeply disturbed by the horrors he witnessed during the war as an ambulance driver and orderly during the Blitz. His paintings of 'Sweetness and Light' betray the underlying turmoil that easily erupted when provoked by the revelations of the popular press and media.

He was born into an age that was secure and predictable and outwardly expressed elegance and order. Its passing left him deeply disturbed and reclusive but he never attempted to portray the changed post-war world in his work, rather he continued to express the joy of flowers and wild animals that brought happiness to millions through reproduction. Only in his later years did his original works find a market. For one so able and so gifted, I have no doubt that his paintings will, one day, command much higher prices. It is all the more remarkable that he kept himself from the income received from reproductions of his work for there are few artists who achieve this. We were indeed fortunate to have enjoyed a long and successful friendship and business association.

Julian A.C. Royle,
January 1987.

Reproduced by courtesy of W.R. Royle Ltd.

It is a sad fact that Vernon's 'commercial' background and his almost legendary reputation in his own lifetime as the originator of hundreds of popular prints and greeting cards, made a number of galleries as well as the governing bodies of the national artistic institutions and societies, reject Vernon as an exhibiting or suitable member. It seemed that no amount of talent, training and experience could compensate for the fact that his name appeared time after time on the bestseller lists of every reputable fine art printmaker.

The first person to cast aside such absurd snobbery and accept him as the true artist he was, was Noël Napier-Ford formerly of the King Street Galleries, St. James, who gave him his first London one-man Exhibition at this prestigious venue which, at last, set Vernon's feet firmly on the road to becoming what he called a 'real' artist. Noël Napier-Ford writes:

VERNON WARD
A Personal Recollection and Tribute

Although my recollection of Vernon dates only from the last nine years of his life, I got to know him very well. Our first meeting was at the King Street Galleries in 1976 by which time he was already afflicted by a severe form of arthritis. However, he could still paint and was full of fun; with Becky acting as chauffeur he was able to undertake a painting trip to the West Country. In the event it proved more onerous than he anticipated and was the last occasion he painted out of doors. In the following year I presented his first ever one-man Exhibition. This was held at the King Street Galleries and was a tremendous personal success for Vernon. I shall always remember the obvious and genuine delight he showed as visitors to the Exhibition expressed their appreciation. The event had afforded him the opportunity he had longed for and the public to see what he could do. Many of the paintings exhibited had already gained popularity through reproduction but the original work had hardly been seen. In 1978 a repeat performance met with repeat success and led to later exhibitions outside London at Chester and Derby.

In the course of preparing the London Shows and acting as co-ordinator for the ones in the Provinces, I became a frequent visitor to the studio in Hampstead. What fascinating visits they were and I can picture Vernon now as he worked at his easel. He never sat down to paint even though standing for any length of time had become a painful endurance. Somehow he would support himself with a stick in one hand, brush in the other, paints on a table nearby, and conjure a magical flowerpiece. Never the tidiest of people, Vernon would drop discarded sketches and scraps of paper on to the studio floor and as he nearly always had the electric fire at full blast it was a miracle that nothing ever caught alight. It was in circumstances such as these that two of the best pictures Vernon made in his later years were painted. I refer to 'Sail Away' and 'Treasure Trove', both commissioned for the King Street Galleries but later sold to Solomon and

'Treasure Trove'.   *Reproduced by courtesy of Solomon & Whitehead Ltd.*

Whitehead Limited and very effectively reproduced by them. The paintings recapture the Edwardian era that Vernon felt himself to be part of and I know they represent memories of his childhood and seaside holidays. They also display a lightness of touch and imaginative treatment which is remarkable when one thinks of the extent to which his hands had become distorted.

Besides having the enjoyment of Vernon's company during my visits to the studio they were occasions when I was able to get to know the very wide range of his artistic skill. Initially, there was the host of work stored away but quickly this supply diminished as paintings were bought at the various exhibitions. Nevertheless, there was always some new surprise as another box of sketches or folio of studies was unearthed. Having started painting professionally at a very early age, Vernon had gone through a number of different phases; illustrations for books and periodicals, history painting, wild life pictures, landscapes and flowers. It was interesting to discover the extent to which he worked larger pictures from preliminary studies and it may be that some of these are a better testimony to his art than some of the highly finished paintings where Vernon undoubtedly had the publisher in mind. He always loved pure landscape painting and in the mid-'forties and early 'fifties had made many small oils, painted on the spot at Sudbrook Park or in Scotland or the West Country. On the other hand Vernon's prodigious visual memory enabled him to compose with great facility imaginative pictures such as 'Final Instructions' or 'Presentation at Court'.

Always a delightful and generous host, Vernon seemed to have a special knack with the very young and I recall so well the times when, together with my wife and three sons, I was invited to Studland Bay for Sunday lunch. They were relaxed and happy occasions with clock golf and walks on the beach. Often the visits were extended to include supper and Vernon must have retired at the end of them quite exhausted. He had been a regular guest at Studland Bay for a number of years, usually in the Spring and Autumn, and the surrounding Purbeck countryside appears frequently in paintings by him. It was also in the beautiful gardens of the Hotel's owners that he gathered much of the material for his flower studies and the management and staff had become accustomed to the temporary conversion of bedroom into makeshift studio. Vernon worked in gouache on these holiday trips as the medium presented fewer practical problems and he could lay out the studies to dry as he did them or, sometimes, they would be strung round the room, suspended from clothes' pegs. For us on our periodic visits, it was a joy to watch Vernon creating with a few deft strokes, that illusion of space and depth which is a distinctive feature of his work.

Looking back in time is something in which Vernon often indulged himself and amused his guests and it therefore seemed natural to choose the words as the title for a small retrospective exhibition at King Street in 1982 but, sadly, it turned out to be his last set-piece show. The illness he had struggled against so long and so bravely was taking its toll and the physical effort involved in making a painting was too much. For those close to him, and one thinks particularly of the devoted Becky, the sight of this struggle and the memory of happier times was a painful experience. Also none of us will forget the agony Vernon endured over the signing of two limited edition prints, 'Swan Majesty' and 'Flanders Poppies', published by Daleguild in 1984. Vernon was in hospital by then and very weak so it devolved on Becky to ferry small batches of prints to and from the hospital so that he could sign them. It was sheer guts that enabled him to finish the job.

In the time that I knew him Vernon demonstrated courage and professionalism in the face of physical adversity and, whenever one met him, a wonderful sense of humour. He is remembered as a friend as well as a business associate and I am fortunate to be included amongst those who knew him personally. For me he lives on through his paintings.

Noël Napier-Ford

'Flanders Poppies'.

'Swan Majesty'.

Becky has mentioned Kay Jones of the Beckstones Gallery in the Lake District and the happy professional and personal relationship with Vernon that followed the initial meeting in Ealing. As usual with those to whom he was particularly drawn, an interesting correspondence developed and, oddly enough, some of these letters as well as illustrating the immediate rapport that drew Vernon to the Jones from the first moment of acquaintance, tell us yet more about the life and character of this enigmatic artist himself.

To quote just a few from a sizeable collection. . . .

Dear Kay and Hugh,   September 7th, 1978

Thank you for your kind hospitality after the 'talk' at the Ealing Art Club. I enjoyed it all so much and the slackening of the natural tension and effort after the 'talk' was a joy. I was very impressed not only with your charming home but with your painting.

With a little channelling of your undoubted talents and being more selective as you are doing now, your inclinations and natural bent seems to me to be emerging from what you have seen and followed to what it is now — yourself emerging so excitingly.

This is normal and, if I may venture to say, the time has come to paint less and draw more and, most important of all, to reflect, to think more. For instance, the new found talent for dog portraiture. If you use a larger board and leave the subject vignetted, the result will be far more enhanced. One learns this 'presentation' by seeing how others have done it and then adapting (*not* copying) this knowledge to one's own self-expression.

I will talk about this if you wish when you come to Hampstead — Becky is arranging this meeting soon, I understand. We are both going away so it should be soon. I hope Royles will be interested in some examples of your work — we must try. Holidays have to be finished with of course, then they tend to consider the next year's requirements about November. We can talk about this over dinner.

What a lovely home you have. I contrast it with my own, inherited of course, huge, unwieldly and, let's face it, downright ugly — 1873 period. Outside the cars stand forlornly, crude in their colours. Sadly they drip little tears of oil, abused (like women), they struggle to do man's bidding. Do they, as they wait humbly to serve their proud, arrogant masters, wonder at their birth? I do wonder at mine. Do they have a shuddering, intuitive dread knowledge of their fate? Once so shiny, once so treasured, then in their old age a liability, a repair bill.

No wonder they crouch on all four wheels, the ghastly fate drawing nearer. The breakers' yard, the cries of metallic anguish as the monster lifts them swaying and drops them on the crunching apparatus.

Let's look to brighter things, to Cumbria, to sheep on the fells, to old England, the England I wanted to paint. Lovely, beloved England.

Have fun, see you soon.

Very sincerely,
Vernon.

Your sweet and generous letter has just arrived. I had no idea you painted in such a lovely satisfying way — so utterly sane in such an insane world! Heavens, what would you have accomplished if you had been completely free? Yet... yet, I feel you have found what I have missed, 'yourself'. I always felt that, the first time I saw your work, but I never have that feeling. Perhaps I have been over-trained, certainly I was far too young to develop what you naturally have.

Oyster catchers.

While I think of it, the breaking wave with oyster catchers came from a half gale on Shell Bay — Studland Bay. There is a deepish channel up which the Sealink and big tankers come into Poole harbour and, whilst waiting for the ferry, the charming little birds with their familiar call were surprised by a huge wave and nearly swamped. Studland is a wonderful beach and in the summer (when I was very young), I was stupid enough to fall in love with a lady, too old for me really but it was my first, and we used to swim there. Youth is always flattered by an older woman and she was an opera singer (Carl Rosa). I was very hard up, my father had died (1926) and we used to use her old Morris Cowley, hang blankets over the 'windows' — sort of cellophane things — and I would plunge in.

She was the Matron of a private boys' school in Southbourne and had I been older and not frightened by my father over sex (or three years in the life class which takes the edge off things!), it might have been different. My father used to say women's strength lies in man's imagination — not true at all but we all need a make up of some sort.

Anyway, I never forgot the breaking wave and the oyster catchers. 'She' had to go to Johannesburg and, heavens, what tears I cried! A last week-end in Tenby where there are puffins and gannets and oyster catchers — I still painted and I have a photo of a very grave young man dreading those last few hours. How strong is the urge to record and how very female I was since she knew so much and I absolutely *nil*. I don't think I know anything *now* except that a Creator must exist and that I do want to be a mermaid (in my next life) and sit on my lovely

Here at last and Freedom. Topless and no need of a Chastity Belt

hair; I think I can get on with other girls and Neptune only likes crab and shrimps for tea. As a 'new girl' I shall have to wash up but at least I won't have to wear a chastity belt! I hope I have a 36″ bust and cup D for easy movement and to aggravate the sailors! It will make a lovely change and with moisturised lipstick etc. all should go well. I hope!

You must sign your paintings more boldly, you are much too modest and people cannot read it, many stick them into books, etc. There are a thousand ways of painting pictures and television has enlightened as well as confused people. Nearly everyone has the germ of art in them but let it die as other things occupy the mind. If one need not earn a living by it, then the artist is fortunate but, oh, to live by it without a patron... If I ever get to write my memoirs, the title will be 'Never Again'. Yet once in a while a painting comes off and its like being in love — all is forgotten and man is so essential especially on moonlight nights.

I think Pembroke became a favourite haunt of mine for wild birds and certainly the Norfolk Broads gave me my love of swans and wild flowers.

I know I can never capture nature in all its lovely variety. You write about it so well and it is sad to think that, even where you are, people will interfere, cats soon find a nest and so on. I'm glad you took to Noël, he really is a discovery and he can write and stick to the point which I never can. I am old enough to love poetry now, I begin to think the written word is all enduring, hence the great masters only uttered their wisdom. I feel you are going to have a happy life for you are away from the rat-race and can stop and stare.

I have to have blood pressure taken and all sorts of things but I am really on the mend. It was sweet of you to write and it cheered me up to have one of your cards. If you ever want to be a mermaid, I'll reserve a place for you or arranging flowers on the Temple could suit you. I'm sure I was a Vestal Virgin long ago and I suppose I listened to some big chested man and got thrown out as being untrustworthy.

I'm sure its nicer being a female than a male. They cannot do their hair differently or try on new dresses. The only trouble is *other women!*

Have fun and don't forget your signature being bolder for printers — they hash up everything.

Regards to Hugh. I hope the northern air suits him and I knew you would like Noël.

Very much love — Vestal Virgin type, of course. Nurse is waiting with syringes and things —

Yours ever,
      Vernon.

Dear Kay,   January 25th, 1980

Thank you for writing to me. I utterly agree that June is a far better time for the Exhibition — Becky will do all the arranging and keep in touch with you.

Regarding the advertising material, I think some of what Noël Napier-Ford wrote may be helpful as he put it so well to the London people. I will say this about myself so you can arrange the information as you feel best since the Midlands and Cumbria *do* know my name but, alas, only by Christmas and greeting cards. It is to broaden this that I am interested in the northern part of the country seeing the real Vernon Ward as well as the well known one — like Daz or Persil!

I was born in 1905, the son and grandson of antique, and especially picture, dealers...

There follows the familiar story of Vernon's early life, all five pages of it, concluding:

I'll send any more information you may want but there is the story of my life which I find fascinating as I look back on it. It is like a dream, it all seemed so rosy in my youth but, alas, when my beloved father died, I began to touch reality. It is good to know reality really for life on earth is not just making money or swindling the Inland Revenue or just being a decent, honest person. There are questions one has to ask oneself sooner or later but that is one's own philosophy and we have to deal with the selling of pictures.

I hope with Becky's aid to come up with enough work to make an interesting show for your new venture. I hope it will be successful but don't worry if things are difficult, I'm well used to that by now. If it were that easy we would all open art galleries and, in any case, you are an artist in your own right. I hope you get over your teething troubles and can then enjoy the lovely countryside all around you.

Please remember me very kindly to your nice husband — a tower of strength indeed.

I am working on some of my lakeland pictures and some of Wales which I love; also hope to paint some Scottish scenes such as I have been selling in London at St. James.

All my best wishes for a happy and successful and, above all, an interesting life.

I feel sure once the winter has passed you will emerge like me, renewed and ready for battle. Bless you both and see you both in June.

       Yours very sincerely,
       Vernon.

June 28th, 1980
                        Lucrecia Borgia's House,
                                 Poison Avenue,
                                     Last Hope,
                               Much Lingering,
                           Hampstead, N.W.3

Dear Hugh and Kay,

Firstly — to thank you both for *all* you have both done for me — not only in selling my parlourmaid pictures which are as dear to me as a woman in a new dress, 'see-through' bra and very lacy knickers (that will shock you!), but for letting me see your lovely home. How I wish I could roll on that white carpet — naturally as a beautiful girl, 38 - 25 - 36!! Ah, what it is to be old!

Still, I met you both so my Star of Destiny is rising.

We had a lovely run back — got home by 6 o'clock and after toasting you in gin and tonic, went and had a huge dinner and as S. Pepys Esq. would have said... and so to bed, where I slept mightily soundly and was only awakened by the chambermaid getting out of my bed at 5.30a.m. since my wife was away with her mother!!!!

Altogether a good time was had by all and I feel mightily refreshed (gave the chambermaid a half guinea and she was satisfied in more ways than one!).

I enclose a story or two for your leisure moments and there is no hurry to return them. Also they are not private so if you think any one else would like to read them, please feel free to let them do so. I shall write lots more as my brain is teeming with ideas.

I thought you looked simply wonderful in the dress I brought and if you ever want to borrow it when you are penniless and shivering in the snow, let Vernon come to your rescue.

Don't forget your [corset] and your [bustle]

and your chemise → (please note built up shoulders)

and your dress improver →

(oh to be a woman now that 1890
    is here)

and your 4 petticoats!

P. S. you'd be surprised how comfortable these can be if you persevere!   Lots of love and xxx.

P P. S. Don't let Hugh see these - he'll get ideas ////

        always and very gratefully yours
                        Vernon.

at Hampstead,
Thursday, August 28th

My Dear Kay,

How lovely to receive your letter which I hasten to answer. How sad that the world is so nasty — I hope the Gallery does not suffer.

Down here it is very dull, a strange gloom prevails like a woman whose housekeeping money has been cut down. My poor garden struggles on — a rose here and a bud there. I did some ironing yesterday; believe it or not, it always has a soothing effect on me. I had washed out (a pitiful exhibition of whiteness over ordinary powders!) some handkerchiefs, a pair of pyjamas and other unmentionables and the light being bad, I went into my kitchen and got to work with an electric iron. As the creases go, so do my problems and I expect you remember that I am training to be a parlourmaid in my next life.

Especially dusting 'real' Vernon Wards, with great care, of course...

Your second cheque was marvellous. Becky pounced on it to pay bills, income tax, VAT, and all the things which depress me so much. She is in Obersdorf in West Germany at the moment and I have asked her to bring me back a woodcutter's doll with a black velvet bodice and a little apron, to go with my Teddy Bear (Bertie O'Knickerous is his name) who looks lonely when I sit him up on my bed! I took him to a hotel — Knoll House, Studland Bay — where I am very well known, and the girls who turn down the beds always put Bertie in my pyjamas. It's a standing joke at the hotel, me and my Bertie.

See what a batchelor is reduced to!

The success of my Exhibition has completely altered my attitude to work. I never knew the northern folk and their kindness and friendliness makes me realise that what I paint is much more understood up your way than down here and I sometimes despair of getting publishers to do anything. I hope you will like the winter. I know it is your first venture but you are out in 'real' country. The winters here are too horrible to my way of thinking.

I am getting going on 'Victoriana' as I believe it is liked up north. So it is here but not in the same way and having done a Cornish harbour scene and touched up some flowers, I now feel free to see if

Cornish harbour scene.   *Reproduced by courtesy of Solomon & Whitehead Ltd.*

I can capture 'that first fine careless rapture!' I am already working on a small figure of a lady writing out a 'list', 1875 period, and her hair and dress is most interesting.

Anyway, you did me a power of good and I loved it all — I think you will settle to a real life. I only wish I had had the courage to get myself a small cottage years ago and lived in the country, worn a sunbonnet and pegged out lines of washing. Of course I should have had a baby and a mythical husband who got lost climbing the face of the Eiger in Switzerland but I became a boy and had a mother to look after me and my three other brothers went off and got married and left me on the shelf.

So, at 75, it is too late except to dream which I do and hope for better luck next time. I hope I get a good place with two other maids and a cook and a butler to do the silver! No pictures to paint, only aching feet and into bed after the washing up — no wonder I paint parlourmaids so well, I'm half one already.

Is Hugh enjoying it? He ought to after the City life.

What with elegant ladies, maids, sea-birds and flowers, I only need a baby to keep me fully occupied. I could tell it fairy stories of bad wolves who wore grandmother's nightdresses and had big ears sticking out as well as a woodcutter's daughter who took her grandfather's lunch of bread and cheese and goat's milk to him every day while he cut wood to earn a meagre living so she only had one pair of d . . . . . s and two petticoats, very patched and darned, and a black velvet bodice to keep her very fine cleavage together.

You know the rest. How 'H.E.' came riding by and asked for a glass of water which was all she could offer him and even that was from a well. Still, they did live happily ever after which is why I like fairy stories because only the good people live happily ever after and the bad old witches turn into property developers and have six telephones on their desks and no time to enjoy themselves.

Dear Kay, I must not ramble on but start work. May all our dreams come true — there's a full moon tonight and I hope it shines on you and Hugh.

Bless you both and thank you.

Always yours,
　　　　　Vernon.

October 13th, 1980　　　　　　　　　　　　　　　　　　at Hampstead

Very dear Kay,

Your lovely card and your kind wishes as well as all you have done for me has been so appreciated. You have achieved a miracle in getting a splendid reproduction of your lovely bowl of pansies. It is terrific, far better than I have ever got them to do, and I send you a thousand congratulations. You must have a magic touch for that is not an easy picture to print as well as Royles have done.

The birthday was simply lovely. I spent it in West Sussex with Becky and another of 'my girls' as I used to call them when I was an ambulance section leader in 1940-45 at Richmond. Of course the three of us got on marvellously and the weather was unbelievably perfect; I was able to limp up to a strange little church which lies hidden in the trees and looks as if it was one of those fairy tale places made of gingerbread and chocolate. Late Michaelmas daisies and dahlias and trees heavy with apples brought back my Edwardian childhood so vividly as I walked up a cottage lined lane and remembered the artists who saw old cottages with women wearing sunbonnets. Artists like Birket Foster and Helen Allingham who gave me lessons in watercolour years ago — about 1910-14 believe it or not.

Give my cheerios to Hugh and once again many thanks, more power to your elbow and congratulations.

ALWAYS yours,

Vernon.

'The Long Bridge'.

Reproduced by courtesy of W.R. Royle Ltd.

May 1981   In Darkest Hampstead

My Dear Kay,

Thank you for the perfect write-up by the very clever Edna Cass. How well she writes and how beautifully expressed. You do live in such a lovely place and I am privileged to have met many of your friends.

Little did I think when I first met you after that talk at the Ealing Art Club that you were going to influence my last years on this swirling, twirling planet. I have grown to love the sturdy clean Midlands and the rugged grandeur of Cumbria with its sincere people who seem to like what I do.

Becky telephoned to say that you have sold some more of my work. How inspiring this is! It is like a woman being respected and needed. I have no great hopes of the Derby show but it is all coming to make sense at the last.

How I wish I had the smooth appreciative ability of Edna Cass. Fancy being able to put into words such colour and even more miraculous she never strays from the point whereas I can never stick to anything. I love things too much. I hope, also I think, that at long last that which we endeavour to paint is a mirror of our inner selves. So I go from wild flowers for which I have a passion, to the joyousness of Victoriana and some of my Edwardian youth. The fact that we do turn over and over now has a reality that I failed to grasp. Had I made cakes, I think I would have learned that everything is a question of probing deeper and deeper.

I shall always see you smiling in the dress I brought at the dinner we had together. Oh, that I had met you fifty years ago but, like Talleyrand, I had to survive in order to learn that which a certain lady once said to a very young worldly '. . . not by appointment do we meet our joys, they try not our expectancy. But round the corner of the street of life they of a sudden clasp us with a smile.'

I was twenty-two then yet even as I burnt my fingers, I have remembered her words, so long, long ago. My first heartbreak and it ought to have opened my eyes to the Real Self, but 1926 came with the hungry men from Jarrow and decent men who came back to a changed and chaotic world.

So hail to you wondrous creature. Destiny worked as it does in its own good time.

My warmest wishes to Hugh and certainly my love to you for a thousand delicate kindnesses,

Bless you always and always,
                                        Vernon.

There are many letters in similar vein. One can only be thankful for Kay Jones, not only for bringing such tremendous joy to Vernon's later years, but for joining Noël Napier-Ford in introducing a whole new world to the masterly elegance and skill of the original works hidden for so long under the plebian mantle of reproduction prints. At long last Vernon was able to enjoy the sort of 'real' success he craved and, with it, a brief foretaste of what was to come, an inkling of what possession of an original Vernon Ward was to mean to posterity.

His later letters to Kay were so sad, the more so because no such sentiment was intended. I have seen this so many times — the end of the road for an artist with so much more to give, mentally as creative as ever, but overcome by the physical handicaps of anno domini, and nothing depresses me more. Vernon's brave words cannot hide the suffering behind the shaky handwriting.

"When Becky told me you had sold a little more of my work, I was truly delighted and also very surprised as I did not think you had any more to sell. It is an understatement to tell you how very grateful I am for this 'out of the blue' surprise. I am in an awful mess with this rheumatoid arthritis and unfortunately the pain killers just do not seem to act upon my body any more. What I am going to do in the future, I just dare not contemplate.

"I write this with odd wriggles to ease my hip and other ghastly pains, the worst of which is that my body feels so heavy . . . like lead!

It is a very nice nursing home and everybody does all that can be done but there is something about this disease that is baffling . . .''

A little later, in March 1983:

"Your snowdrops must look heavenly. Have you tried a bunch in a blue and white bowl or just a little gathering — sort of vignette? One can always back them up with some dark ivy leaves and the effect can be most attractive.

"I scribble this with the utmost effort and I am sorry (and amazed) to say everything is over now as far as I am concerned. Every type of treatment has been tried with no effect . . .

"It will be lovely up your way soon and I am happy to know that you have other artists and that you are in such good form. Do phone Becky when you can — she is a dear to me and so are you. I hope Hugh is fit up in your lovely Beckstones with the water rushing at the back of your lovely home.

All my love, always,
Vernon.''

19 June 84

Dear Kay and Hugh
            Thank you for your good wishes.
I do hope you are enjoying this lovely
weather . It is nice down here too and

The nurses are firm but very efficient. My asthmatic has finally let me down and I try to do a lot of reading. Will you forgive a very tiny brief note? My hands are wobbly and my thoughts very confused. I loved your card. More power to your elbow.

I hope Hugh's asthma is better and the Beckstones is at its usual lovely rushing stream.

I need hardly say that Becky has been a tower of strength.

She is so kind and good — I wear her out with endless fears and my memory has gone to pot.

With happy memories of you in 'yr chair

        Yours
          Vernon.

Enjoy every hour.
I have to guess your address as I have no address book.

'Country Décor'.   Reproduced by courtesy of W.R. Royle Ltd.

Lastly, at least within the limits of this book for I have received many personal letters and telephone calls from admirers of Vernon including fellow artists who have been inspired by his work or helped in some way by personal contact or his written word, I quote from Jackie Myer, now living in Salt Lake City, with whom Vernon was a close (pen) friend. It appears to have been rather a unique and unusual relationship between two equally unique and very individual characters.

Jackie Myer writes:

I think I may have first met Vernon Ward in the early days of World War Two, in 1941 or possibly 1942, but I can't be absolutely sure. My memories of that time are hazy and perhaps I only imagine that we met because my great friend Laura spoke of him so often. Laura and Vernon worked together in the Richmond Civil Defence and, from tales she told me, I certainly formed the impression that here was a fascinating and different sort of person; an artist who painted flocks of wild fowl flying over desolate marshes (I think I saw some of Vernon's pictures at this time and they were always of birds) and who claimed to spend each night on the Astral Plane from which vantage point he looked down upon his fellow workers tossing on their narrow bunks and described their every move to them in the morning! Laura also told me that Vernon believed in reincarnation — a brand new concept to me — but which meant, I discovered, that he would one day be 'reissued' in a brand new body and go round again as somebody else! All this sounded highly intriguing and when I went to live in America after the war, I still had news of Vernon from time to time in Laura's letters. He was a well known artist by then and painted other subjects beside birds. Somehow, he always remained an entity in my mind throughout the years, if only because he was a friend of Laura's and in some queer way another link with home. I little dreamed he was to enter my own life forty years later in a rather unusual way.

In 1967 I began making regular visits to England, usually two years apart, but it was not until 1979, forty years after our real or imagined meeting, that we met again and he asked me to write to him. He said he needed a 'pen-pal' as he put it and I volunteered to oblige. I never imagined at the time what a fascinating, frequently bewildering, but always intriguing assignment it would turn out to be. Really my whole knowledge and impression of Vernon Ward is founded on that correspondence. For roughly six years we exchanged letters fairly frequently and when one of the big envelopes with the Hampstead address in the top left corner would arrive, I'd drop everything, pour myself a sherry, and settle back to wind my way through yet another of these most unusual letters. And unusual they certainly were! That he wrote them at all is remarkable because, at this time, arthritis was crippling his hands so that he could hardly hold a pen. Already they were bent too much to hold a brush and I wondered what more terrible fate could have overtaken an artist. No wonder waves of despair broke through at times; I felt his pain, both physical and mental in the words he wrote. There he sat in the big old house in Hampstead where he was born, confined for the most part to his chair, living out the long days with his memories, regrets and fears for the future, unable to relieve them even for a moment with the work he loved. But they weren't whining letters — far from it. They contained much humour, much chivalry and much thought provoking discourse on the meaning of existence and the truth or falsehood of the world's great religions. Sometimes I must admit, he had my head reeling by including Buddha, Krishna, Lao-Tse, C.S. Lewis and Billy Graham in the same paragraph! And when he threw in references to the gods and heroes of ancient Greece, he sent me running for my Edith Hamilton. He certainly was an avid seeker after truth and seemed to have adopted bits of this and bits of that, blending them into an astonishing composite all of his own. As for chivalry, that was directed at me and I admit I found it a pleasant fantasy. I must have told him in a letter that I was haunted by the colour orange for the next envelope arrived addressed to 'Madame la Comtesse l'Orange' and they continued in that vein. He even called me his 'silver greyhound' — alas, no more — and when he discovered I was a June-born moon child, he decided I was Artemis and instructed me on the proper ceremonies to observe when the moon was full!

By the time we had been exchanging letters for half a year, I realised that Vernon was a highly complex and many sided individual. I also knew that at least one side of his nature was pure romantic. He yearned for a past he remembered and, just like his favourite poet, Omar Khayyám, who he quoted in almost every letter, he obviously longed to 'shatter this sorry scheme of things entire and remould it nearer to the heart's desire.' In one letter he included a sheet on which he had recorded his turbulent emotions while watching a film of E. Nesbitt's 'The Railway Children', a story he remembered from his childhood. ''My heart seemed to burst in agony'', he wrote, ''as I saw again the fields and the wild flowers, the 'gone forever' peace of the villages, the steam train, the porter, the important old gentleman, the Mother, the long skirts, that formed part of my childhood. I am seventy-five now and terribly disabled but, oh God, my memories. The swagged mantelpieces, the maids, the gas-lamps, the iron and brass-framed bedsteads, the utter innocence of the children, yes, innocence, which I shared as I watched this remarkable film.''

He went on to deplore, a favourite theme, the planners and property developers who ''are bringing ruin to our England''. Much of what he wrote on that sheet, I felt great sympathy with. Certainly our age creates runaway ugliness at every turn and Vernon loved beauty above all. One can scarcely be an artist without that. Was the Edwardian age of his childhood really so much more innocent? I don't know for I hadn't yet arrived here but Vernon obviously longed passionately for the innocence of that gentler world he thought he remembered.

The last time I saw Vernon was at Twyford Abbey, the home in which he spent his last days. He seemed bitter and withdrawn, perhaps not without reason, for he had had to give up his old home and darkness clouded his mind. I left England hoping this final phase wouldn't last long. To see the soul of an artist shut up in a disabled and distorted body is hard to look upon. The deep love he had revealed to me for the beauty of the English countryside and all that sensitivity to light and colour had been reduced and confined to a barren room and a strip of terrace outside. I was thankful when the news came from England that he was gone. But curiously, he suddenly seemed very near and I couldn't figure it out. I'd only known him for such a short time and that through letters, yet the weight of his personality seemed hanging in the air and would not go away.

One day in early summer, a few weeks after he died, I was drowsing under my apple tree thinking of nothing in particular, when a huge and gorgeously painted butterfly swooped down upon me and continued to make seemingly deliberate passes over my chair again and again. Suddenly I heard myself say, ''Why, hello Vernon! How lovely that you're free at last and all the pain is gone.'' A fabulous fancy? Well, maybe, but then again, maybe not. Perhaps for a moment the spirit of Vernon really did inhabit the body of that beautiful butterfly and he had come to tell me that he was free at last and that all was well with him. At least I hope that was the message.

My own memories of Vernon Ward before the discovery of our shared affection and admiration for the late Anna Zinkeisen were simply impersonal and professional; it was as I progressed with the customary biographical research for this book that I found I was getting to know him as a person, retrospectively, but very well. Twenty years ago, I should have been very surprised indeed to learn that we had so much in common — but then this book is not about me!

I have called his an enigmatic character which is true but, at the same time, I feel that I have actually known him in the flesh and, in a way, have for him a very strong sympathy — perhaps empathy would be a better word, Vernon would not have appreciated sympathy in its accepted sense, nor would I have offered it.

Something like a quarter of a century ago, I was handling Vernon Ward prints commercially but I must admit that, at the time, I was fairly indifferent to the majority of them although I could understand their popular appeal. As a painter myself and becoming more and more involved with original works generally — prints were prints! However, as the standard of reproduction began to improve so enormously, and particularly as I became familiar with his original work, my ideas about Vernon Ward changed somewhat. I gradually became more and more aware of the talent, craftsmanship and skill behind the work of this singularly underrated painter and to be able to relate the quality of the original to the reproduction, visualising the real painting behind the printed page.

Looking at Vernon Ward's original work, particularly the flower paintings and the Edwardian subjects, one is immediately struck by three things.

Firstly — the joy of creation which shines through those magical flower studies and the Edwardian compositions, painted just because he wanted to and because they took him back, for the time, to an age whose passing he so deeply regretted. Vernon has, through such paintings, become known as 'the painter of sweetness and light', the light that can only be communicated through the intangible medium of love and joy in every brush stroke. Vernon Ward was passionately in love with beauty — beautiful flowers, the English countryside, the sea and sea birds, butterflies, attractive, beautifully dressed women be they duchesses or maidservants — and to love one's subject so intensely is the essence of beautiful painting. Vernon has spoken of the flower as "loveliness incarnate" adding, "to love the flower is to love God; it is as simple as that. Why not seek this Kingdom that is not only all round but within us?"

There is an interesting little side story, related in a way to this, which explains the reason for certain of his work appearing somewhat less inspired by such sentiment! Outside of the strictly commercial work, advertising, illustration, and the like, when Vernon was asked to paint something he did not want do do, "soppy" pictures as he called them, out of which he would gain no aesthetic satisfaction whatsoever, he refused to sign himself 'Vernon Ward'. For such occasions he took on the name Bertram Linder, abbreviated to B. Linder, and these became known as the 'Belinda' paintings.

Two of the despised 'Belinda' paintings.   *Reproduced by courtesy of W.N. Sharpe Ltd.*

Vernon Ward with a more characteristic work.

Secondly — his handling of paint and the sheer skill of his brushwork, a factor not altogether apparent when looking at reproductions unless the manner and style of the painter's original work is familiar. Large brushes and generous use of paint are not generally associated with such delicate work, made to appear even more so by the inevitable flatness of even the best reproduction, yet Vernon manipulated both with extraordinary dexterity. Of the assortment of brushes held in his left hand like a bouquet — he preferred not to hold his palette but to rest it on a table beside him — his favourite was a 2½ inch varnish brush with which he would not only lay in his background and larger areas but often use its chisel edge for such fine lined detail as stems and branches or the rigging of of a ship.

It takes an accomplished hand to perform such tricks just as it does to lay on paint as heavily and sensuously as he did, then deftly transform it into a perfect flower or whatever, blending in the high and low tones, sometimes simply adding pieces of pure pigment to catch the highlights. Any area of a painting that did not please him, even good painting that he decided spoilt the overall composition, was summarily rubbed out with a paraffin rag and repainted; unlike many lesser painters, no matter how much scrubbing had gone on, no one was ever aware of it in the end result.

His father's wisdom in encouraging him to copy from the works of many and diverse masters had helped to perfect all these techniques and more; add to this his inborn, very considerable, talent, the sort of enquiring mind that is determined to work out how the many and various effects and results have been achieved, with the tenacity not to abandon a copy until this has been done, and we have yet another answer to the versatility and formidable skill of the much maligned Vernon Ward.

Thirdly — to take up the point touched on by John Ward, R.A. in his foreword — the magic ingredient, certainly the one that ensured his popular appeal and made him a not inconsiderable income however much he may have felt that it was not making him a 'real' artist.

For Vernon Ward knew how to paint for reproduction without undermining the quality of the original painting — his unerring mastery of tonal values and the understanding of how they would reprint, whether intuitive or born from experience, gave him the edge over so many who have tried in vain. As John Ward points out, painting simple everyday subjects accessible to any painter and making of them not only beautiful pictures but extremely decorative prints which brought in handsome royalties, it might be expected that a plethora of aspiring artists would strive to imitate him.

I know of a number who have — and no doubt there are many more who have tried and found it did not work for them — they just did not have that magic ingredient that adds light and life and that certain intangible 'something' to a handful of hedgerow flowers or a tiny corner of rural England, still less to be sure that the same qualities will be recognized in reproduction form. For many who have felt they were on the right road and submitted work for publication, back comes the rejection slip from a publisher who knows that, unlike the Vernon Wards, their colour contrasts, tonal values or general composition will not make a satisfactory print.

It can be said that there are hundreds of prints and greeting cards by contemporary artists, but believe me, these represent only a small proportion of work submitted, and of these, how many have had the constant or constantly repeated success of Vernon Ward? One thinks, of course, of Rowland Hilder or the Johnstone twins but they, too, are of the old school which is dying away.

Vernon Ward seemed intuitively to know what would reproduce well, an unrivalled combination of intuition and experience with no suggestion of contrivance at the expense of the original. One of the saddest things about his life is the fact that this very skill made him an outcast, a 'commercial' artist not to be granted the entrée to the more prestigious galleries (until Noël Napier-Ford took the plunge) or professional bodies because he had 'cheapened' himself. No wonder that, as he became old and ill and no longer able to paint, he became very bitter and resentful. Just as the tide had turned and he was finding recognition and success as a 'real' artist, the pernicious arthritis took over, destroying his life both physically and mentally.

For the rest of us, though, he lives on and as time goes by his place will be assured. The decline in standards of traditional academic painting in recent years will only serve to highlight those artists who really understood how to draw and paint without resorting to gimmickry to attract attention.

It seems sad, too, that Vernon leaves no family of his own to take pride and pleasure in belated acceptance and appreciation of his work. He loved his friends dearly and they reciprocated, showing in many cases, a very real gratitude, kindness and affection. Yet it is easy to see why Vernon never married — he was far too much the hermaphrodite, in many ways far too much a woman himself ever to marry one. He admired, revered and respected women and had many women friends but more probably because of his affinity *with* them than any desire *for* them. He never recovered from what he saw as a sex change when he was 'breeched' and part of him always hankered for the feminine life, if possible lived in an Edwardian era where time would stand still.

I see Edward Fitzgerald as his literary parallel, another man 'with friends possessed', whose friends were all, and whose abortive, unconsummated marriage to Lucy Barton was a short and dismal failure. Fitzgerald's genius was for long unrecognised and unacclaimed, while now he is held in great esteem and biographical publications are legion.

I think Vernon would have liked being identified with Edward Fitzgerald; both were brilliant men who had all too little recognition in their own lifetime, and both were charming, amiable eccentrics. *The Rubáiyát* appealed to Vernon, too, so let old Omar quash his patronising and disparaging critics —

"Pish!

He's a Good Fellow and 'twill all be well."

Appendix

A small selection from Vernon Ward's prolific writings which possibly provided an outlet when arthritis limited his painting.

"IN THE MIDST OF DEATH"   9 November, 1977

In this age of swift revolutionary changes in the once all powerful but now discredited Church of England the social unheavals are sending established thought reeling back from entrenched positions that in past times went largely unchallenged.

A religious system that up till the end of the Victorian era held fast to principles (outrageous when considered in cool, logical reasoning) is now in complete social disarray. The concept of Christianity, supposedly emanating from the teaching of Jesus of Nazareth which was reputedly recorded by his disciples who were 'educationally' illiterate in the times of the Master, was bound to lend itself to the struggle for men's minds. There was bound to be conflict over what was originally said and what the translations inevitably altered. Our moral attitudes, i.e. Christian ethics, have been based upon Jewish history.

The condensed sayings, all translations of translations in the Bible itself, undergoing yet another 'interpretation' to fit into current language, are now in open conflict with present day socially changing attitudes. One of the greatest changes we see in present times is that of the position of women. In Biblical times her place was firmly in the home — the handmaid of Man. In Genesis man was created first... Adam as the symbol of mankind was in existence long before Eve. It was only his failure to be satisfied with the companionship of his Creator that led to the creation of Eve. If this account is only symbolic of mankind's attempt to explain human creation surely it were wiser for the now tottering Church to come out openly and revalue its teaching. Either Genesis is true or it is not.

The Darwinian theory (and it still, to my mind, remains only a theory) explaining nothing of real importance except the unbelievable credulity of man who seems to accept almost anything, clashes hopelessly with the concept of Christian belief in God endowed by man with man's limitations, but the very claims of the Roman Catholic organisation — so hotly disputed today — are, to my mind, fantastic, as I think are all the other religious systems. This is not to postulate atheism. I do not think man can ever abandon his belief in his Creator. For his 'creation' is a fact. Darwin tries to explain the presence of the most superior animal on this planet by a vague theory he calls evolution. I for one can no more accept this silly postulation than I could accept the Roman Catholic teaching that they and they alone know the actual Will of God.

The Americans are very fond of the term 'self-evident' so in spite of my own reservations that nothing is what it seems except decay, death and birth, I will use this term to say that the revaluation of all religious systems as interpreted by man is long overdue. The almost complete breakdown of moral values and the utter disregard for established laws can only end in such chaos that man will destroy himself as surely as if he could explode by his scientific discoveries in the nuclear experiments he is now busily engaged upon. If man ever discovers a planet containing an entirely new form of life, then we shall be confronted with a self-evident fact that will utterly overturn the rickety ideas now held by man. The religious forms of expressing worship and obedience to one sect is of no importance to another system. There are millions who believe the 'Messiah' is yet to come, and to come, moreover, from the body of a male! Hence the wearing of a specially cut garment to catch the falling new-born child.

There are others who believe they have the power to absolve sins — sins which are crimes so horrible that decent people reel away in horror. Those who decimated millions of innocent Jews under conditions of such fiendish barbarity can only be compared to two foul murderers still alive on this earth who actually recorded on tape the cries of the little children being experimented upon. (There exists a group of people who would actually free these ghastly inhuman things to dwell, in a subhuman, carefully concealed existence as outcasts of society, and who actually expect the parents of the murdered children to forgive these 'animals'.) I mention this case which is sadly, only one of many to illustrate the unbelievable attitudes held by man.

The long bloodied record of the Church's terrible intolerance towards the religious beliefs of others which led to the invasion of the Holy Land (the Crusades, as this form of brigandry was termed) now sounds like some nightmare. The cries of the tortured in dungeons of so-called Christian Europe fill my heart with an unutterable sadness at the devil existing in man — in men robed as monks, priests, bishops, popes and prelates.

I could quote, if they be true, the utterances of the very Master's Son (only Son of God made flesh but nevertheless perfect) Jesus, who was reputed to have said to his disciples that "Evil must come: but woe unto him through whom it comes" (evil exists and therefore it has to be) and he goes on to utter one of the most terrible warnings to those who practise such horrors. . . that it would actually be better if "the doers of Evil had a stone, a millstone put around their necks and then cast into a bottomless sea". Krishna, the great god of another religious system says that evil ones will be spewed out of evil wombs over and over and over again — getting more and more evil. Can man think up a more complete Hell than that so solemnly prophesied by these two Great Teachers? Yet man believes differently. The cruelty continues, the persecution still goes on. What can man do now? He is utterly lost. That is the Truth. He still thinks a few new laws, and pressure for so-called human rights will solve his appalling dilemma. Yet his vices, his cruelty, his bestiality, his sexual foulness and his frightful greed is worse now because of the great forces of his inventiveness: the bacteria, the nuclear missiles, the hellishness of his exploring, obdurate brain and above all, his capacity to 'fool' himself all of the time.

The dogs of war are loose with a vengeance. Lands are claimed, the planet hustles on endlessly as its inhabitants glare with bloodthirsty eyes at each other. Blackmail is rampant, no one can walk in any degree of safety. Contemptuously the young flout the very law that is designed to make their situation upon this earth a decent, safe (as far as possible) existence. The fact is Man does not believe in God. If he did he would not behave as he does. If he really did believe in law, in the idea that God cannot be mocked and decided that as he sows so shall he reap, he would not attempt to do the contrary. But he does not believe. That is what is truly self-evident.

The prisons are filled with people who have tried to 'get away with it'. They have lied at their trials, they have fallen for bribes, for greed. They have deliberately exploited their fellow men. These people are adroit, glib and no doubt many are never, on earth, found out. Their crimes go unpunished. Upon their deathbeds they confess of them, and are calmly given a full and free pardon for a life of sin and vice and corruption of others. They come out of prison unashamed of what they were punished for, and appear on television presumably for a fee, or write unabashed their account of their infamy for the newspapers and expose more corruption for large sums of money. How Jesus would be sickened at what is called civilisation in the world today. In our own country man fights man with a grim determination worthy of the best traditions of the Inquisition. New laws are designed to subjugate the law abiding, taxes levied to support unwieldy enterprises, and the very Church is working deviously to undermine countries that hold differing views. They have learned nothing from their past atrocities. They are forced to accept the other religions now being firmly established in this country, ironically by their own Christian beliefs. That these 'alien' beliefs are adhered to and practised with a devoutness far beyond the fast failing Christian belief is again self-evident. The ultimate fate of the newest religion could possibly be as final as the fate of the Red Indian in America. Wherever conquering man has gone he has eliminated all opposition — join me or else. Who could resist the forces of materialism? Man — the so-called conqueror, is himself swept along in the stream of his desires.

Science, which should help man, is his terror. Medical science is getting bogged down with the survival of the 'unfittest'. Heart transplants versus the pill. Seat belts versus bad, lawless, male driving. Man blackmails man. Kidnaps and hijacks. The Priests intone. . "Oh God make speed to save us". Save us from what? From being born at all? From being a thalidomide baby because a woman will not bear pain? To be apparently a victim of man's drugs and be in bed without arms or legs?

Isn't it time that people in high places stopped hiding their heads in well paid buckets of sand and came out, not to be counted (there are too many for that) but to just say what is now self-evident? That they, the ones who argue so learnedly for their own cause, just Do Not Know.

Man cannot think through to anything: he is not to be blamed for that, only asked to accept blame for his irresponsible conduct. When he first invented the motor car he had a man to walk in front carrying a red flag. How right he was to view the first horseless carriages as deadly as a bomb. The effect of the machine upon the human mentality beggars description. It has conquered him... He can no more rid himself of the motor car than he can conquer his ego. He is a slave. Worse still, he does not know it. He actually thinks he is free and postulates (self-evident too) that not only are *all* men born equal, but that all have the right to pursue happiness. (I like the word pursue, as if it were a horse in a field, wary but able to be captured, like a woman.)

The dishonest wrigglings of Churchmen regarding the priesthood being made available to mere females are laughable. They have no more idea why they were born as males than they have of what they will become when they have to die. They could just as easily be born girls. Why not? Or are they the 'chosen of God'?

Within most religious systems women have been trodden on, ignored, relegated to an unimportant position, locked away in harems, and veiled, if they dared to walk in public, as if they were something odd. Women priests? What? — giving the Holy Sacrament! And themselves possibly unclean — Never — not in our lifetime, say the ecclesiastical chauvinists. What is the difference between the spirit inhabiting the male or female body? Like Shylock do they not both bleed if you stick a knife in them? Just because the position of women in Eastern countries including the land where Jesus was born (of a woman, curiously enough) was little better than that of a chattel to be bought and sold, to be used to breed children, to prepare food, and to keep out of sight, she is now, according to the General Synod, not fit to be a priest. I have listened and seen on television a priest refer to Saint Paul as the 'authority' for denying women the priesthood. As if Paul of Tarsus knew anything about women. Paul who set out with two companions armed with a Roman Emperor's certificate to knock the living daylights out of those revolutionaries in Damascus, and no doubt would have done, most effectively, if the voice from the burning bush had not intervened.

How can men be so utterly dishonest? They know perfectly well that women priests will come, as women judges, lawyers, doctors, etc., are now a part of human affairs, and who will say they will be as guilty of the cruelty and bloody murder that male priests have practised for hundreds of years? It may well be that the experience of childbirth and all the sickness and physical disfiguration, real disfiguration (not the Church's idea) and inevitable pain, as well as the glory of actually bearing a life in one's body, could give a compassion and an understanding quite beyond the capacity of man. Who will cast the first stone of denial to women of equal virtue? I very much doubt that a woman could watch a human being hung up by his wrists in a dark dungeon with iron weights upon the victim's feet to enhance the agony and watch impassively as the cowled monk must have done in bygone days. What price hijacking? If people want films of horror, of torture, of violence beyond belief, may I suggest a true version of the activities of man as in the dungeons of the Inquisition, the water torture, and the filling up of the orifices of the body with cement? Why invent stories when the truth might bow the heads of those watching with shame and fill the obdurate heart with a remorse that would bring the tears at last to the blackened soul of mankind? How can man ever progress to his Creator when he brushes his terrible conduct under the carpet of self-interest? Why dress up in stole and surplice, clamber up into the pulpit and continue with an outworn, outmoded form of worship that by its very wearied mechanical lifelessness is unconvincing to a nation hell bent upon destroying its soul, polluting its possibilities? Why not thunder against Evil and forget the forgiveness of sins? Leave that to God for it is, after all, 'His' business.

Concentrate on the chaos, the barbaric vandalism, the judges who will not judge, the magistrates who will not try to use their small powers. Thunder against those who are in power and are openly and deliberately making life so wretched for the innocent, the old, the frail and the helpless. Are there are no islands far North where the antisocial, the proven villains, the corruptors, the rapists and loathsome murderers can be kept to themselves, to live the life they evidently want? Can society not say to these antisocial ones — You care nothing for us and our laws... therefore we care nothing for you? Go from our sight — become what you wish to be and live and fight it out amongst yourselves — we reject you as you have rejected us. Our children shall not see you nor your own, be you male or female.

Those who wish to preserve you and save you may go freely to the Island of Devils. They can be landed to live among you, to try out their experiments, to be the missionaries no doubt they honestly feel themselves to be. What better than to work among these impossible people? It is their choice. But we do not want them to experiment with the honest on this earth. Inflict the murderers, the rapists, the God forsaken, upon those in society who claim the right, the human right, to reject. To at last say — enough is enough, you are no longer welcome. Man will have to learn. It is self-evident that what he is up to now is leading straight to destruction and real death. The Death from which there is no pardon.

"FAREWELL TO YOUTH"   19 October, 1977

There is an ache in my heart as I sit in the Swanage bus trundling its load of old people, I making one of them, to the old seaside town that nestles so logically between the steep white cliffs. And as we descend the steep curving road past the many little private hotels there is the beach.

I never pass along this tiny esplanade but I see with my nostalgic eyes the Swanage of long ago. I have a book of photographs of Dorset. Old photographs they are, with its inhabitants and the summer visitors crowded happily upon the sands. Girls in their teens with summer hats upon long hair hanging freely over young shoulders. Young children, hoops in hand, stare at the beach players singing on tiny canvas stages — the deck chairs filled with an Edwardian summer audience. The sweet pain in my ageing heart is because my own holiday draws to its inevitable end. And when one grows old as I am growing old the 'inner eyes' see something that busy ardent youth happily cannot see. Everything is so precious, for Time — that hour-glass of my life — is warning me to look keenly at all I love so much, have loved so faithfully over the many years I have visited this unspoiled part of Dorset. A sweet ache, a pang of pain, for I have but one more day. I was born in October, long ago in 1905; I have seen and I have felt life's 'Winds of Change'.

I see in those old photographs all those vanished people, young and old, now gone. We had our time as all who are born to live have their brief hour. The smell of the seaweed comes strong from the beach as I stare at the same scene, same in essentials, only the costumes are different and there are no bathing machines. The children dig, the parents relax in deck chairs and the seagulls patrol upon lazy wings the edge of the oncoming tide. Dogs chase each other and splash about in joyous tail-wagging freedom. I remember, and softly hum, that well loved tune . . . 'Oh I do love to be beside the seaside — I do love to be beside the sea . . .'

Old as I am, with arthritic bones twingeing as I lean against the bus stop awaiting the red single decker, I too still love to be beside the magic of the seaside. An October day, warm and misty and the white cliffs are soft in pastel colours as they melt into the gentle sea. With a loud hiss of the opening doors of the bus I pull myself up and pay the return fare and make my way to the empty seats at the back. Others clamber up, struggle in, parcels, plastic shopping bags hugged upon short-skirted laps or trousered ones, blue-rinsed white haired plump ladies returning to those modest hotels. Like myself they are having a last holiday before the stealthy winter will keep us indoors with our memories. As we wind up the long steep hill the Dorset scene unfolds in its gentle beauty. The black and white young heifers, tails swishing, cluster near the mellow hedgerows, hedgerows that in May were white with cow-parsley and bright with the new spring gold of buttercups. Now, like the people in the photographs they too are gone. Russet and yellow leaves line the narrow lanes and the bracken is warm upon the hills.

The sharp black and white of a magpie flights across the bus as it grinds slowly up into open countryside. Autumn is here, in its full glory. The cottages we have passed flame with scarlet dahlias and the rich symphony of the Cast of Autumn Flowering is in its vivid beauty. I delight as always in this brave assembling of the full beauty that is so much a part of our English inheritance. My life, my earthly life, is drawing to its gentle decline. Why is there an ache in my heart? It is because I must leave for my own home where there is little country and where the horizon shows the sprawling city of London, hideous as seen from Parliament Hill. Grey tower blocks rise up like silent monsters overseeing the swarming struggling creatures who are caught in their own apathy.

Here in the Dorset lanes I have felt the reality of life, delighted in the late butterflies heedlessly flighting upon beautiful wings to settle upon Michaelmas daisies or cream coloured dahlias. Nature is dying, but it is the gentle death heralding the resting period until once again the hedgerows are a spatter of tiny green buds upon dark twigs and small brave spears of green thrust upwards to renewed life. I am filled with gratitude that I have seen and felt this endless miracle for so many years. Now it is becoming more urgent for me to see it, for I am seventy-two, over man's three score years and ten.

My work as an artist, my deep love of my country and my humble strivings to depict what I have felt so deeply as I have seen the varied scenes of the most beautiful country in the world, have given me the reward of a new and deeper spiritual vision. I have loved my country with all my heart, with all my soul and the Great Goddess Nature has given to one of her many worshippers a pair of bi-focal glasses, for I can stand and see the Heavens in all her beauty as John Constable the painter saw the skies. I can stand in the moonlit scene and see the starlit canopy over me and feel at one with Eternity. The silvered disc we call the moon exerts its magic call specially to me as it does to those in love.

Looking down through the bi-focal glass I see the life going on amid the leaves and blooms of this autumnal scene. A late bee clambers into a dahlia and a ladybird hastens out, a tiny spider bravely commences to spin a tiny web, a pale green caterpillar swings slowly down on an invisible gossamer strand seeking a safe place wherein to hide throughout the winter, safe in its chrysalis shell to emerge in early spring, a veritable example of reincarnation. There is a vast world of creation going on in the space of a few yards. I lift up a large stone and I disturb a whole multi-creatured colony. The sunlight sends them racing for the shadows, and I replace their stone canopy. We are all creatures existing upon this planet we call Earth.

Entering into it from the womb of woman we have an allotted time to grow from the helpless baby into our Destiny. Why? Why all this wonder of Creation, all those tears, the ache in my yearning heart for the reassurance of my Creator? It is so vast, too big and as I grow older I see that man knows nothing. He has his courage, and his ignorance sustains him, but the old can see with different eyes if they wish, for they can look back. They revalue and they see it all as a play, for they have acted their rôles upon a shadowy unreal stage. Soon the curtain will fall upon the last act — the lights will go out — the play is over.

Is the ache in my heart because I see so much now in the fruition of my years? The old should not cling overmuch to life upon this planet. We know (or should, if we think it through) that change is life. There is no real Death, only a passing from one state to another. That other, if we have lived well and in purity and honesty, must be finer, where the soul has nothing to fear, where the spirit is freed from the confines of the physical body with its inevitable heritage of change leading to the Autumn of one's own earthly life. To die is to live. To live is to die. Is it all pointless? I do not think so. I lift up my eyes to the stars. Who put them there? Who gave the spider the know-how to spin its web to survive? Who set the teeming life upon the earth — who set us spinning in space? Why create man and woman with their immense possibilities and their ability to reproduce themselves as surely as the 'ear of corn'?

Man is the only animal that can doubt. He can also reason. He can say that 2 and 2 makes 4. He can deduce from that a great hidden truth. For that is a Law. By that 'Law' his own physical body was made in the womb of woman. Man forgets that but I do not think woman ever does. Man is not only incredibly ignorant, he also ignores. He has had Super Teachers come from time to time to show him by their example the possibilities he has within him, but he forgets his brief time upon his schoolroom — Planet Earth. Foolishly, like greedy children he claims it as his own, parcels it up, pollutes it, quarrels over it and goes to war to get more of it.

The wise grow old and stand apart and in the Autumn of their time they leave this turbulent earth never to return, and the young inherit their own time and continue to quarrel, love, fall down, get bruised and try to dominate each other — kill each other as animals do — are forced to do — for Nature knows no morality, has no conscience. But man has, stifle it as he will. The mystery of his being is ever beside him as the seasons are enveloping him. His ideas are absurd — his courage immense. Like his childhood his toys occupy him to the exclusion of his contemplation of his Destiny. The rewards are so eagerly sought. The price paid so impossibly high. For man has an ego. It drives him on and on, often to disaster, always to agitation. He cannot leave off. His desires, whatever they be, drag him down into the dirt where he wallows in unseeing complacency. The old know better. Age is a stern teacher. It is not mocked. As man sows so he must inevitably reap. The tragedy of man is he secretly thinks that this is not so, that he can reap and say — ''after me — the Deluge''.

But the curtain falls, the players leave the stage and the lights go out. Only the night watchman is left to go the rounds. For there has to be a night watchman. Man's behaviour makes that necessary. As his behaviour makes his birth necessary. In the womb he develops in utter darkness and if he ignores, as so often he does, the nature of things, he will return to that darkness. For that too is the Law.

The Planet spins in its destined space, it orbits the sun. The night must come and the day must dawn upon the other side. This circling is man's inheritance implicit in his life. End and beginning have to be one. There can be no straight line for man, only growth. To grow is to live. Death is the ceasing to live. Yet in Death is Life. Like the green tiny bud upon the tree. It will become a leaf and in the Autumn it will fall in its golden time, gently and slowly, as mankind will. From the decaying leaves comes the leaf mould so necessary for rebirth.

It is 'Why?' that man cannot answer. If he could he would be God.

THE END